CHRISTIAN LIVING
IN A PAGAN CULTURE

Christian living in a pagan culture

Douglas D. Webster

Tyndale House
Publishers, Inc.
Wheaton, Illinois

Library of Congress
Catalog Card Number
80-51700
ISBN 0-8423-0241-7

To my wife, Ginny

CONTENTS

PREFACE

The long yet worthwhile route to publication has convinced me that many Christians are eager to examine the meaning of their faith for their daily lives. Whether we like it or not, reader and author alike have long since been immersed in a culture which conditions our thinking on everything from the television and interpersonal relationships to the family and materialism. The contemporary culture has become a multifaceted curriculum, instructing us in the ways and means of life in the eighties. This book was written to challenge some of the basic assumptions and habits promoted by our pagan culture. To do this we turn to God's Word, the only adequate antidote to programmed conformity, and we seek to "read" our culture in the penetrating light of Scripture's in-depth analysis and insight.

This book began with a group of adults, mostly middle-aged, in a suburban Chicago church. Benefiting from their interaction, I was spurred on to deal with the subject more thoroughly. Teaching a course at Ontario Bible College while doing graduate work at the University of Toronto provided that opportunity. This book would never have been completed without the help and encouragement of my wife Ginny. During the months I

interrupted my doctoral work to write, her daily routine
consisted of working by day to support us and typing the
manuscript at night.

The reader has a challenging task ahead and may deserve
credit in advance. This is not a how-to book. I attempt to
avoid pat answers and model solutions which encourage
the reader to copy rather than to think. The book is
intended for serious Christians who seek guidance in the
joyful struggle of living fully and freely for Jesus Christ in
a world which by nature and practice stands in opposition.

D. Webster
Easter, 1980

ACKNOWLEDGMENTS

Quotations from *Archaeology and the New Testament* by Merrill F. Unger, © Copyright 1962, are used by permission of Zondervan Publishing House.

Material taken from *Christ the Controversialist* by John R. Stott, © Copyright 1970 by the Tyndale Press, London, is used by permission of InterVarsity Press, Downers Grove, Illinois.

Material taken from *False Presence of the Kingdom* by Jacques Ellul, © Copyright 1972 by The Seabury Press, Inc., is reprinted by permission.

Excerpts from *Future Shock* by Alvin Toffler, © Copyright 1970, are reprinted by permission of Random House, Inc.

Quotations from *Images of Man: A Critique of the Contemporary Cinema* by Donald J. Drew, © Copyright 1974 by Inter-Varsity Fellowship of the USA, are used by permission of InterVarsity Press.

Excerpts from *New Testament History* by F. F. Bruce, © Copyright 1969 by F. F. Bruce, are reprinted by permission of Doubleday & Company, Inc.

Quotations from *Peace Child* by Don Richardson, © Copyright 1974 by Gospel Light Publications, Glendale, California 91209, are used by permission.

Material taken from *Rich Christians in an Age of Hunger: A Biblical Study* by Ronald J. Sider, © Copyright 1977 by Inter-Varsity Christian Fellowship of the USA, is used by permission of InterVarsity Press.

Material taken from *The Scientist and Ethical Decision*, ed. Charles Hatfield, © Copyright 1973 by Inter-Varsity Christian Fellowship of the USA, is used by permission of InterVarsity Press.

Material taken from *The Social Economic History of the Roman Empire* by Mikhail Rostovtzeff, © Copyright 1957, is used by permission of Oxford University Press.

Quotations taken from "The Socialist Quest for the New Man," by Josif Ton, *Christianity Today*, 26 March 1976, are used by permission.

Excerpts from *What Is a Family?* by Edith Schaeffer, © Copyright 1975 by Edith Schaeffer, published by Fleming H. Revell Company, are used by permission.

1

THE NEW MENTALITY

May this mind be in you, which was also in Christ Jesus [Philippians 2:5, KJV].

First-century Christians obeyed the commands of Christ in a radical, life-transforming way. They demonstrated to the world a new way of living. The Church experienced sin and failure, but one thing was clear to the watching world: discipleship meant a complete reformation. The whole of life came under the revolutionizing impact of Jesus Christ and the authority of the Word of God. Standing today in the twentieth century, we cannot help but be impressed with their struggle to confront the mentality of their pagan culture with the Lordship of Christ. Oftentimes their faith brought society's harshest judgment. Poverty, persecutions, and even death resulted from taking Christ at his Word.

He who does not take his cross and follow after Me is not worthy of Me. He who has found his life shall lose it, and he who has lost his life for My sake shall find it [Matthew 10:38, 39, NASB].

The disciples demonstrated then what is true today: "there is not one religion for the Holy of Holies and another for the common life."[1] The Word of God exercises complete authority over every area of life. Both our worship and our work are equally important in God's eyes. We have been *given* a new identity and a new reference point from which to operate in the world. All that is to follow in our discussion of the Christian in the modern age is pointless if we do not know for a fact that God has made us new men and women.

Probably no other period of history has known such an intense preoccupation with the question, "Who am I?" Experiencing an identity crisis seems to be an almost automatic prerequisite for maturity in the modern world. Ethics, morality, life-style, vocation, and a host of other factors are determined by modern man's number one consideration—self. Finding one's self is the prescribed formula for discovering some jag of meaning upon which to hang one's life.

The new mentality has a different starting point. The crucial question is not "Who am I?" but "Who art Thou?" The Apostle Peter did not follow Jesus in order to find himself. He followed because he believed. "You are the Christ the Son of the Living God." Jesus' response gave Peter a new identity. It affirmed his individuality ("You are Peter . . .") and assured the permanence of his self-worth and self-responsibility ("upon this rock I will build My Church"). Like Peter, we have received what only Christ can give us. We are "new creatures" because Christ has made us new. Jesus' response to Peter reveals the utmost love and confidence he possesses for the Church. If we fail to live up to our true identity, we have betrayed Christ's trust. The disciple's new commitment is not a negotiable contract. We can not debate or lobby over the terms of the agreement. Christ bids us to come and *die*. In return, he entrusts us with everything the cross stood to gain. The new mentality begins with this one simple fact, "if any man is in Christ, he is a new creature; old things passed away; behold, new things have come" (2 Corinthians 5:17, NASB).

This book is an attempt to wrestle with some of the issues confronting us as Christ's followers in the twentieth century. It is addressed to all who take seriously their new identity and are willing to face the challenge of being all that Christ meant them to be.

I am deeply concerned that in many ways we are vulnerable to the mentality of the modern age. Hardly a Sunday morning goes by that I do not feel deeply frustrated. I sit with men and women who share the same Christian convictions as I do, but we are aliens within our church. We belong to Christ, but in so many areas our way of life belongs to the world. We sing the hymns, listen to the sermon, give our offering, and wake up to find a Monday morning world staring us in the face. Are we prepared to live as Christ's distinctive, called-out community? I am not a prophet of gloom, but I am a firm believer that little is to be gained by ignoring our failure to cope with the present situation. We have so much to gain by allowing the Holy Spirit to develop in us a Christ-centered life-style. If true believers fail to offer a positive and constructive resistance to the modern mindset and life-style, we will continue to see the breakdown of our families through divorce and parent-child conflict. We will have little resistance to the tremendous pull of materialism upon our lives. We will continue to be shallow and aloof in our relationships with fellow believers. We will subject the world to an impersonal, programmed approach to witnessing. We will compromise our ethical conduct and morality. We will stand in silence while the world cries out in need. We will respond halfheartedly to the gospel mandate to go into all the world and make disciples. We will look with innocent indifference upon our Third World Christian brothers.

At this point you may be ready to close the book and say with a sigh, "This man is just too pessimistic for me." Believe me I am not trying to turn you off, but I am convinced that the conditions of the North American evangelical church are far more serious than we wish to acknowledge. If we do not sense our need, we will not be motivated to prayerfully and thoughtfully evaluate the issues raised in this book. There are many books which deal with a particular aspect of how a Christian should live in today's world. For example, a book on the family or missions. My purpose is different. I have attempted to bring together a comprehensive overview of the Christian's role in culture. This is a blend of theological and

historical perspectives on specific cultural issues. None of
these important areas has been dealt with in its
totality, but all have been approached from a biblical
perspective. I hope the style and content will achieve its
intended purpose of strengthening the twentieth-century
believer in his daily life.

If this book stimulates and guides believers and their
local churches to grapple with the pressures and
promises of the modern age, its purpose will have been
achieved. It comes down to this one searching question,
"What does it mean for the Christian to live in obedience
to the biblical imperative, 'Do not conform any longer to
the pattern of this world, but be transformed by the
renewing of your mind'?" (Romans 12:2, NIV).

2

WHO IS CHRIST?
WHAT IS CULTURE?

WHO IS CHRIST?

Jesus asked his disciples, "Who do you say that I am?"
(Matthew 16:15, NASB). As they stood face to face with
Jesus there was no way to ignore his question. They were
called on either to affirm or deny his Lordship. The nature
of his question was dynamic and personal. Confessing
Christ as Lord is no one-time altar call, but an ongoing,
costly commitment. Whether we realize it or not, we answer
this question, "Who is Christ?" every day of our lives.
The scope of the question is so great that the answer
embraces all of life. Our daily actions either serve to
demonstrate or deny the true identity of Jesus.

Before Jesus asked his disciples, "Who do you say that I
am?" he questioned them about the popular opinion, "Who
do men say that I am?" The disciples responded, "Some
say John the Baptist; some, Elijah; and others, Jeremiah, or
one of the prophets." Certainly these were great men who
figured substantially in the history of the people of Israel.
They were used by God to reveal his will and shape their
culture. But Jesus made a division between the popular
opinion and the disciples' personal conviction. Jesus
asked, "Who do *you* say that I am?" and Peter responded, as
the disciples' spokesman, "Thou are the Christ, the Son
of the Living God." Peter's confession moves us from the

realm of public opinion into the realm of spiritual insight.
"Blessed are you, Simon Barjona, because flesh and blood
did not reveal this to you, but my Father who is in
heaven." Peter's confession expressed the true identity of
Jesus in contrast with what was commonly accepted.

How does the modern world define Jesus Christ? If Jesus
were to ask us what he asked his disciples, what would
our reply be? For eight months I taught at Chung Yuan
Christian College in Taiwan. Many of my students were
from a completely non-Christian environment. They
understood Christianity as a strictly Western
phenomenon, imported along with Western commodities
and technology. Christ to them was nothing more than a
Western Buddha or Confucius. This example may place the
problem far from home, but you can understand the need
and difficulty in separating the cultural image from the true
identity of Christ.

More immediate examples can easily be found. Take for
example the teenager whose ideas of Christianity are
bound up in his parents' church: a building, meetings, and
young people's group. When put together this forms his
impression of Christ. Or the politician who looks at the
church and sees the great silent majority and concludes,
"This is Christ." Or the theologian who in his support of the
aggressors of socio-political liberation in Africa and South
America boldly declares, "This is Christ." Or the
"fundamentalist" who relies upon his Christianized
legalism, his dos and don'ts, and responds with assurance,
"This is Christ."

Culture has been in the business of defining who Christ
is ever since he placed himself in the midst of our world.
There is no lack of cultural images intended to represent
Christ, but these temporal, stop-gap answers only belittle
the Son of God. The Christian must guard against
superficially responding to Christ's question, "Who do
you say that I am?" When worship becomes only a habit of
our tradition, and obedience is little more than
conformity to others, we are in the process of reducing
Jesus Christ to a cultural image.

The Israelites in Jeremiah's day considered themselves to be the people of God. They worshiped in the temple, sacrificed in accordance to the law, and listened to the priests, but they did not know God. They were a religious people, but not a spiritual people. Standing in the temple gate, Jeremiah declared the words of God:

Do not trust in deceptive words, saying "This is the temple of the Lord, the temple of the Lord, the temple of the Lord." For if you truly amend your ways and your deeds, if you truly practice justice between a man and his neighbor, if you do not oppress the alien, the orphan, or the widow, and do not shed innocent blood in this place, nor walk after other gods to your own ruin, then I will let you dwell in this place [Jeremiah 7:4-7, NASB].

Knowing God meant responding to life's situations in a way consistent with the character of God. But the Israelites failed in this, willfully permitting the materialism and syncretism of the surrounding cultures to control their lives.

If we are to respond to Jesus as Peter did, "You are the Christ, the Son of the Living God," we must live in conformity to the character of Jesus Christ. "Who is Christ?" is answered not only with intellectual conviction, but with a changed life-style. The believer is *of* Christ—nurtured and empowered by the Word and Spirit of God. The problem comes when the believer's life no longer proclaims Christ; then his testimony is no longer authentic spiritual insight, but a cultural opinion. In the first century, any Jew who compared Jesus to men such as Jeremiah or Elijah thought he was being quite complimentary. Likewise today, the man who considers the church worthy of his attendance and his offering believes he is paying tribute to Jesus Christ. However, in neither case is the Lordship of Christ truly acknowledged. "Who is Christ?" is a vital, demanding question that can only be answered in the power and wisdom of God. It takes us beyond a creed into a living, personal relationship with our Creator and Lord.

WHAT IS CULTURE?

The second question, "What is culture?" follows from
the first. If Jesus is truly Lord, we have a mission to
accomplish and culture is the arena. In later chapters we
will study particular areas of culture, but first we must
look at culture in general. H. Richard Niebuhr defines
culture as "the total process of human activity and the total
result of such activity."[1] In essence, culture, using the
term in its broadest sense, is our total way of life. Niebuhr
sets down four basic fundamentals for culture.

First of all, culture is *social*. Man as a social being is not an
island unto himself. His language, reason, and personality
are developed in community. Secondly, culture is "the
work of men's minds and hands." It is the product of
human achievement. Niebuhr writes, "A river is nature, a
canal culture; a raw piece of quartz is nature, an
arrowhead culture; a moan is natural, a word cultural."[2] A
third aspect of culture is its *value system*. Values are
inherent in any culture. Total anarchy is never an enduring
condition in society. The nature of man is such that he
requires some kind of standard or value system upon which
to operate. The values that a culture uses may be morally
evil and may be in a constant state of flux, but they are
values nevertheless. Finally, Niebuhr suggests that
culture is *pluralistic*. The world around us is built and
sustained around diverse and often conflicting interests.
Culture is always in tension, each man working toward his
own success, sometimes for the good of culture and other
times for its destruction.

These four characteristics of culture show us the
collective consciousness of man. Culture is not a product of
time plus chance, it is a product of man who is made in
God's image with personality, reason, and moral
consciousness. Fundamentally, culture is more a product
of man than is man a product of culture. And although the
social dimension of culture may come to mean
homosexuality, abortion, and fragmented families, man is
still God's creature. And although human achievement
may come to mean nuclear war, test tube babies, and
political corruption, man is still subject to God's

judgment. And although values may come to mean "if it feels good, do it" or "if it can be done, it will be done," man is still in conflict with his inner moral conscience. Paul speaks of the law written within men's hearts which accuses men when they oppose God's standard (Romans 2:14, 15). And although pluralism may come to mean tyranny, anarchy, and oppression, man is still loved by his Creator.

It should be noted here that there is a parallel between the dimensions of culture and the dimensions of the Christian's life. The Christian operates in the world, but he is not of the world. He has exchanged his solidarity, his oneness in Adam for the redemptive union he has in Christ. The Church is his new social realm, giving meaning and purpose to interpersonal involvement on every level. His achievements are considered in the light of his Christian responsibility and his values are shaped by the Word of God. Pluralism is understood positively in the diversity of function and unity of purpose which exist in the Church. The disciple of Christ has begun to experience, through a genuine relationship with God, a fulfillment of his humanity—a restoration of his true identity as the image-bearer of God.

CHRIST AND CULTURE

Jesus entered culture in a very revealing manner. After thirty years of obscurity, the Incarnate One came to the public's attention. Three incidents comprise this introduction: his baptism in the river Jordan, his wilderness temptation experience, and his first public address in his hometown, Nazareth. Heralded as the Lamb of God, Jesus was baptized by John not because he was a sinner in need of repentance and forgiveness, but because he wished to identify with man in his need. John at first refused to baptize Jesus, saying, "I have need to be baptized by You, and do You come to me?" But in order to "fulfill all righteousness" (Matthew 3:15), Jesus was baptized, identifying himself with man in his need and with God the Father in his redemptive plan. The event is far more profound than a mere indication of humility. This is not the introduction of a folk hero or a religious model. Jesus stands as the one who must radically deal with the root problem in man's existence.

It was Christ's unique position as representative of both God and man that Satan wished to destroy in the wilderness. If Jesus had arbitrarily used his power or opted for immediate success, he would have destroyed God's redemptive plan. On the other hand, if he had defeated Satan by means not available to us and had dismissed man's need for true forgiveness, he would have broken his solidarity with man. Satan was wise in his challenge. He knew the all-embracing historical and cosmological issue at stake. The ultimate defeat of Satan came in the cross and resurrection, when Jesus fully represented man and God by dying for our sins and living for our redemption.

Christ's message in the synagogue at Nazareth was his declaration of purpose.

The Spirit of the Lord is upon me,
Because He anointed Me to preach the Gospel to
the poor.
He has sent me to proclaim release to the captives,
And recovery of sight to the blind,
To set free those who are downtrodden,
To proclaim the favorable year of the Lord [Luke 4:18, 19, NASB].

After sitting down, Jesus uttered these remarkable words: "Today this Scripture has been fulfilled in your hearing." The new age had been inaugurated with the revelation of himself. His presence and his action would make the healing of the whole man possible. Jesus began his earthly ministry by confronting culture. A culture which included man, with all his needs, and Satan, with all his powers. A culture, allowed by God, in conflict with God, and now uniquely confronted by God.

CHRIST AND HIS CULTURAL ANTAGONISTS

Richard Niebuhr summarizes the charges made against Jesus by those who have opposed his redemptive work.

Some have argued that Jesus *ignored culture*. Joseph Klausner writes, "He did not come to enlarge his nation's knowledge, art, and culture, but to abolish even such culture as it possessed, bound up with religion."[3] It must be recognized that to some degree Jesus did ignore culture, especially those areas that seemed most crucial in the minds of many first-century Jews. Jacques Ellul comments on Jesus' political involvement:

One hesitates to bring up the obvious fact, which nevertheless is generally forgotten, that Jesus paid no attention to the problems of politics. He definitely refuses to take the lead in the Jewish nationalist movement. He recognizes the authority of the invader. He advises the normal payment of taxes (which was then a burning issue with the Jews). He displays an indifference toward the question of taxes, showing its unimportance by the story of the fish (Matthew 17:24, ff.). He welcomes "collaborators" and traitors, and at no time does he take a stand against the numerous political scandals which were rampant in Judea. Jesus says nothing against Roman torture, or against crucifixion (of which we know from several examples of that era, that the sentences were sometimes unauthorized!) or against extortion.[4]

Jesus must have frustrated those who, seeing in him the perfect catalyst for political change, envisioned what his popularity could do to aid the zealot movement. However, the segment of society which had the most to lose by Jesus' apparent disregard for culture was the Jewish ruling class. Jesus' indifference to the delicate balance of power between Rome and the religious leaders placed in jeopardy the continuation of the status quo. The Pharisees knew full well that the leeway extended to them under Roman policy could easily be curtailed if they no longer commanded the respect and authority of the general populace (John 11:47, 48). Although some may say that Jesus ignored culture, it can not be said that he was ignorant of these cultural tensions. What really disturbed the Pharisees was Christ's power and authority, his revolutionary approach to the ceremonial law, and his constant association with the despised people of society.

Jesus confronted culture not to destroy man's educational, artistic, and social development, but to destroy Satan's grip on culture. The cross of Christ is always present—in every healing, every parable, every intimate conversation or public address. But then we often become so preoccupied with things in culture that Christ and his cross become secondary rather than central.

Others have offered a second objection saying that Jesus was "other worldly." Possibly the cliche, "He's so heavenly minded he's no earthly good" would sum up this criticism. It is not difficult to understand how critics have arrived at such a conclusion. The Gospels continually report that Jesus looked beyond the human dimension. Surely this must have been Pilate's impression after talking with Jesus. Can you imagine Jesus, the defendant, saying, "My kingdom is not of this world. If my kingdom were of this world, then My servants would be fighting, that I might not be delivered up to the Jews; but as it is, My kingdom is not of this realm" (John 18:36, NASB). But Jesus did not separate the human from the divine, the secular from the spiritual. True spirituality does not exclude the human in order to include the divine. Jesus looked beyond the human. He did so, not as an Eastern mystic who wishes to exclude the human, but as the Son of God subordinate to the Father. He reveals this inclusive relationship in a very concrete way when he said to Pilate, "You would have no authority over Me, unless it had been given you from above; for this reason he who delivered Me up to you has the greater sin" (John 19:11, NASB). God's sovereignty was responsible for even Pilate's authority.

Jesus left no literary, academic, or political achievement. He taught informally for three years, and somehow excited enough opposition to get himself crucified. But such an account is completely inadequate in explaining the historical significance of Jesus of Nazareth. If Jesus had not been "other worldly" he would not have affected this world. His impact upon culture and his followers can be explained only through his divine relationship to the Father. This is his claim and history has demonstrated its truth.

A third objection has been the *exclusiveness* of Christ. The historian Gibbon accounts for Rome's reaction to Christianity. It was to be

expected that they would unite with indignation against any sect of people which should separate itself from the communion of mankind, and claiming the exclusive possession of divine knowledge, should disdain every form of worship except its own as impious and idolatrous.[5]

The criticism that Christianity is exclusive is entirely justifiable. Jesus clearly stated it, "I am the way, and the truth, and the life; no one comes to the Father, but through Me" (John 14:6, NASB). And the apostles faithfully proclaimed it: "There is no other name under heaven that has been given among men, by which we must be saved" (Acts 4:12, NASB). The exclusiveness at issue here is an exclusiveness demanded by the Truth. The Christian maintains that the knowledge, obedience, and worship of God is not arbitrary and man-made, but a matter of absolute truth revealed by God. However the *spiritual* exclusiveness demanded by God is not to be confused with *cultural* exclusiveness.

In Jesus' day, as in ours, there was a great deal of animosity between people. The Pharisees disdained the common man, considering him to be ignorant of the law and crude in its application. Pilate and the Romans looked down on all Jews; Pharisee and commoner alike were subject to them. The political zealots opposed both the Jewish establishment and the Roman occupation. Everywhere one looks in first-century Palestine there were cultural divisions between Jew and Gentile, Jew and Samaritan, male and female, free man and slave, rich and poor. But Jesus cut across those divisions. The gospel knew no cultural barrier. It was intended for all men everywhere (see Matthew 28:19; Galatians 3:28; Colossians 3:11). The Christian is commanded to be culturally inclusive, not in spite of but because of his Christ-centered exclusiveness. He is to be tolerant in spirit, but intolerant in mind. John Stott writes,

We need to distinguish between the tolerant mind and the tolerant spirit. Tolerant in spirit a Christian should

always be, loving, understanding, forgiving and
forbearing others, making allowances for them, and giving
them the benefit of the doubt, for true love "bears all
things, believes all things, hopes all things, endures all
things" (I Corinthians 13:7). But how can we be tolerant
in mind of what God has plainly revealed to be either evil or
erroneous. [6]

Jesus demonstrated spiritual exclusiveness and cultural
inclusiveness in a perfect way. We must ask ourselves if
we, by the power of the Holy Spirit, uphold the truth in love
and liberty, crossing all cultural barriers with a clear
representation of Christ.

   The fourth objection is that the life-style Jesus called
for was *incompatible* with the duties of life. This idea says
that the Christian position is not practical enough for the
real world. Jesus was an idealist. His forgiveness was
incompatible with the legalism of the Pharisees and
meaningless before Pilate's situational ethics. At times
Jesus' words became repulsive. He uttered words like "he
who eats My flesh and drinks My blood has eternal life;
and I will raise him up on the last day" (John 6:54, NASB)
when what the people wanted was assurance of more bread.
Without a doubt, we must say that Jesus' words and
actions were incompatible with culture. The Sermon on
the Mount was not a cultural mandate. It stood for the
opposite of what culture represented. Jesus did not aim at
making men better, he lived to make men new.
Everything that Jesus tells us to do is incompatible with a
humanity still in bondage to sin. Jesus came to transform
men in culture—to liberate them from sin. The cross is the
historic demonstration of Christ's incompatibility with
culture, and yet it is his death on the cross that bridges the
gulf between man's depravity and God's holiness.
   Jesus did not accommodate culture. His true identity
always stood and even now stands in contrast to the
popular opinion and cultural images. In one sense, the
criticisms we have just examined are all justified. Jesus
was not preoccupied with the things which fascinate men

most, and his reliance upon God the Father was total. He demanded the exclusiveness of the truth and was spiritually incompatible with his culture. God forbid if we do not antagonize in a similar way.

3

JESUS CHRIST
AND THE WHOLE MAN

Standing before Jesus was a man very few of us can truly
visualize. His body was torn and scarred from repeated
attempts to break the chains that checked his violence
and served to make society secure. He was a wild man,
naked and unwashed, who haunted the Gerasene tombs.
He was humanity at its worst, but such a description fails
to capture the meaning of the Satanic presence. To this
man Jesus came in the power of his Word and commanded
the unclean spirits to depart. The man objected, "What do
I have to do with You, Jesus, Son of the Most High God? I
beg You, do not torment me." Jesus replied with a
question, "What is your name?" Jesus dealt with this
tormented individual as a man, a whole man. The name
"legion" stood for all the despair and wretchedness this
man had experienced. It was, in a word, his curse and his
identity. Even this man, as despised and dreaded as he was,
had a name. Jesus met this man where he was and brought
about the healing of the whole man. This Gerasene
believer, from any human standpoint, had been an
extremely unusual, pathetic case. But without minimizing
the very real impact of Satan's presence, Jesus saw in
Nicodemus the very same need as he saw in the demoniac
and he met that need in the very same way. Whether we
talk about a crooked little bureaucrat named Zaccheus or

the Samaritan mistress who gave a drink of water to Jesus, we are talking about people like ourselves, who need a transformation in their whole being.

Zaccheus was more than a tax-collector to Jesus. The Samaritan woman was more than an adulteress. Nicodemus was more than a religious leader. These people stood before Jesus as spiritually naked and lacking as the Gerasene demoniac. The demoniac's needs were obvious; their needs were hidden. But in both types of people we see images of modern men and women. Their cultural labels did not prevent Jesus from seeing them as people in need of wholeness. The demoniac was a man with a name, Zaccheus was ministered to in his home, and real forgiveness was possible for the Samaritan woman. It did not matter if a man was a centurion, or a zealot, Pharisee or politician, rich or poor—the need was fundamentally the same—and Jesus dealt with the individual as a total person. Jesus ignored the categories of culture as he met men in culture. His love was not abstract. The good news of salvation was given personally and its impact was immediate and wholistic.

If we compare Jesus' method of dealing with men and women with our own methods, we are brought to the conclusion that our modern mentality has gone a long way in shaping our approach to people. To support this conclusion, I would like to deal with the question, "Who is modern man?" and then discuss Alvin Toffler's "modular man."

WHO IS MODERN MAN?

Modern man is progressive. We desire to be innovative and creative in our approach to the whole spectrum of life. We are open to new experiences and ready for social change. There is, it seems, a constant desire to thrust ourselves forward. In spite of energy shortages, unemployment, and high inflation, we are possessed with a certain modern mood of restlessness which makes us uneasy if we stay too long in one place. This modern progressiveness is evident in the life of a corporate executive who is promoted, geographically moved, and forced to stay on top of technological and economic changes. It is also evident in the life of a child who experiences a constantly changing educational program, a family separated by new cultural standards of morality and marriage, and an increasingly fragmented adult world.

The men and women who receive our recognition and acclaim are the innovators. The people who make the changes, discover new data or resurrect old ideas, and clothe them in new forms. There has never been an age more energetic than our own in acquiring facts and cataloging the data. Progress has become the business of the world. The frontiers of the past were vast stretches of uninhabited wilderness. Today's frontiers are technological, scientific, and anthropological. Man has not set out to conquer the land, he has set out to conquer himself.

Modern man is contemporary. If indeed we are a people possessed by progress, it can also be said we are a people of the present. Modern man is concerned with the *now* of time. Our clothing, language, automobiles, and political policies reflect our persistent preoccupation to be current. We plan for the future, but the future is seen as nothing more than an extension of today, and the past in many respects is despised. To some degree man has always been concerned with the immediate and less concerned with things in the past or future. However, there is a growing realization that more than ever before, modern man is both shaped and enslaved by his incessant desire to be contemporary. In other words, the young adult may seem to exert a tremendous impact on life-style, but in fact he is being manipulated by an older generation interested in commercial gain. In appearance he is a victor; in reality, he is a victim. Another example which places the modern concept of time in perspective is that we no longer associate norms of behavior with absolutes that stand outside of time, but we allow time to dictate the norms of behavior. Certainly this has been true to some degree at any point in history. However, never before has society so overwhelmingly oriented itself to a relative standard.

Modern man is affluent. The chief motive for living appears to be the use and accumulation of wealth. We are first and foremost consumers. This is no new fact. It can be argued that there is very little difference between the man who fights for survival and the man who lives for pleasure. Essentially they are both materialists. But what is especially characteristic of modern man's affluence is that he has chosen *things* over *people*. No longer do we envision security and happiness primarily in terms of human relationships and our relationship to God. People become functionaries only as valuable as the dollar value of the task they perform. Affluence has led us to a very real sense of isolation. We are imprisoned by things, related to one another through things, brought together on account of things, and separated because of things.

Modern man is enlightened. Advances have been made by modern man in world relief, labor relations, mental-health care, and political reform. There is a growing understanding of minorities and an appreciation for social reform. With these and other advances has come the confidence that man is able to achieve a measure of success in dealing with social problems. In principle, tolerance is the mental mood of the enlightened man. Truth has become a subjective matter, defined in relation to changing times and personal opinions. In reality there appears to be little tolerance for the man who holds to absolute truth revealed by God in the Bible.

C. S. Lewis exposes the critical deficiency of man's enlightenment:

Niceness—wholesome, integrated personality—is an excellent thing. We must try by every medical, educational, economic, and political means in our power to produce a world where as many people as possible grow up "nice"; just as we must try to produce a world where all have plenty to eat. But we must not suppose that even if we succeeded in making everyone nice we should have saved their souls. A world of nice people, content in their own niceness, looking no further, turned away from

God, would be just as desperately in need of salvation as a miserable world—and might even be more difficult to save.[1]

Lewis's statement brings us back to man's fundamental condition. We are separated from God. Man was made with the capacity to reason, to communicate, to love and be loved, to exercise dominion over creation, and to worship and obey his Creator. Yet all of man's capacities were twisted by the Fall. Man became self-serving and ignored the living God.

The Christian should see through the facade that modern man has constructed. Being progressive, contemporary, affluent, and enlightened may paint a positive picture of today's man in the eyes of most twentieth-century men. But the portrait is abstract and faceless. Man has no personality. He has lost his true dignity. His purpose for living revolves around that which has no true reference point. In our attempt to conquer the world we have become increasingly less certain of our own identity.

THE MODERN MENTALITY—A COVER-UP

The gospel can only be received when men and women sense their need. Good news is not even news to people who are no longer listening. But the Christian must realize that behind that beautiful abstract painting of modern man stands a Gerasene demoniac, a Nicodemus, a Samaritan woman, a Pilate—men and women who have faces, who were made by God in his image. Although often it is not realized, the need for God and for forgiveness of sin is intense. The hollowness of our age has served to accentuate that need, even if it seems covered over by an appealing life-style.

On several occasions I have been to the Pacific Garden Mission in downtown Chicago. The men and women who come in off the street bear all the marks of degenerate humanity. Their minds have been affected by drugs and alcohol, their emotions are shattered from loneliness and

depression. There is no indication of success, only failure.
Their drawn faces and hollow, bloodshot eyes
communicate to the outsider nothing but despair and
despondency. No one has to be convinced of Satan's
work; it is clearly evident. But to drive north on Lake Shore
Drive along Chicago's Gold Coast, past the fashionable
apartments and wealthy homes, we receive an entirely
different impression. Here is the "cream" of our culture,
exuding all that modern man stands for. But here too are
men and women in desperate need of redemption and
transformation and the Christian is called upon to relate to
them on a personal, wholistic level, measuring success
by those who are truly transformed by Christ and
incorporated into the body of Christ, the Church.

THE MODERN MENTALITY—A COMPROMISE

The modern mentality not only serves to cover up our
spiritual need, it also compromises the Christian's true
identity. As believers we have tended to measure success
by the same standards used by non-Christians. In the
process of fighting for the best of what modern man has
to offer, we have compromised effective Christian service. In
other words, the middle-class evangelical is either
alienated from or indifferent to an inner-city work because
of the cultural distance that stands between himself and
the "lower class." He is also ineffective in his middle-class
surburban environment because he has been absorbed
into the mainstream mentality. Rather than living out the
gospel, he has patterned his existence after the world. We
find included in this abstract painting of modern man the
believer—but a believer who has no face. He has lost his
identity.

Jesus confronted men and women by demonstrating
love and speaking authoritatively. He lost himself in the will
of the Father, not in the spirit of the age. For if he had been
one with his age, he would have had no lasting message.
But Christ's gospel was not conditioned by the times. He
did not reflect his culture. He shaped his culture by
transforming men into his image by restoring them

through justification and reconciliation into fellowship
with God.

Do the Apostle's words apply to us today?

*For consider your calling, brethren, that there were not
many wise according to the flesh, not many mighty, not
many noble; but God has chosen the foolish things of
the world to shame the wise, and God has chosen the weak
things of the world to shame the things which are strong,
and the things of the world and the despised, God has
chosen, the things that are not, that He might nullify
the things that are, that no man should boast before God*
[1 Corinthians 1:26-29, NASB].

Is it possible that the twentieth-century evangelical
believes that he has gone beyond such a description? Is
this still an appropriate picture of the Church? We cannot
afford to deal with such questions flippantly. They spur us
to grapple with basic issues. It is my opinion that by and
large we do *not* identify with Paul's description. We see
ourselves as more sophisticated Christians, representatives
of both the wisdom of our age and the wisdom of God. Far
from being despised by our culture, we expect and often
receive the praise of culture. Could it be that we pride
ourselves on being the epitome of the modern enlightened
man? We are nice people with a special interest in
goodness.

Paul encouraged the church at Corinth to uphold the
truth of God in every domain of life: marriage, money, the
use of spiritual gifts, attitude toward non-believers,
harmony between believers, discipline, worship,
instruction, etc. It was Christ's Lordship over all facets of
life which transformed the Corinthians from the mentality
of their age into a distinctive minority which reflected
the love of Christ. Paul does not mean that Christianity is
only suitable for the lower classes of society. We can not
imply from his description that the Church needs fewer
executives, doctors, lawyers, and educators. But what we
can learn from his words is that the Church must manifest
in every way the wisdom of God and not the mentality of
our age. That will mean that my self-image should be

controlled by my relationship to Christ rather than by my
professional occupation and that how I spend my money
cannot be determined by how much I make. The wisdom
of God, working through the body of Christ, is the only
adequate solution to the deep-seated needs of the
individual who stands behind the faceless, abstract
representation of modern man.

THE MODERN MENTALITY—
THE WRONG INFLUENCE

The modern mentality not only compromises the
Christian's identity, it also influences our approach to
people. We are conditioned to relate to one another
impersonally. Alvin Toffler writes in *Future Shock*,

*We have created the disposable person: the Modular Man.
Rather than entangling ourselves with the whole man,
we plug into a module of his personality. Each personality
can be imagined as a unique configuration of thousands
of such modules.* [2]

If we go to the store to buy a pair of shoes, we do not need
to be bothered with all the personal problems and successes
of the shoe clerk. We only need to relate to him as a shoe
clerk. This carries over into our work. We know people as
they relate to us through their work. Certain modules of
their personality are necessary for us to know if we are to
work with them, but other modules, such as their family
responsibilities and their outside interests, remain
unknown to us. Toffler justifies "Modular Man" on the
basis of a well-ordered, properly functioning society. He
argues that the demands exerted upon us by modular man
are much less than those inherent in traditional
relationships. Therefore man, modular man, is free from
unnecessary restrictions. He is free to get through his
formal, functional relationships and spend time with a few
intimate friends. Learning to live with depersonalization,
according to Toffler, is the practical approach to modern
culture.
    It is immediately evident that we can not establish

wholistic relationships with everyone we meet, but granting that, we must emphasize that the Christian's approach to people ought to be wholistic. The man who is operating according to "modular man" relationships may have the exact same conversation with the shoe clerk that the Christian has. The difference between them lies in the fact that the modular man is truly closed to knowing the clerk as a person. He is interested in him only as a shoe clerk. The Christian, however, ought to be open to the clerk as a person. True Christ-centered openness is no easy task. It demands self-denial and sacrificial love, a genuine responsiveness to those in need. It calls for a willingness to cross the frontiers of selfishness and cultural difference with the wholistic gospel of Jesus Christ.

Truman Douglass in his book, *The New World of Urban Man*, analyzes what happens when man settles for "shallow and trivial self-images." He writes,

This has been the effect of narrowing freedom by restricting the area of choice to choices of life goals and personal commitments. It leads to development of the necessary syndrome in which all other persons—and by implication ourselves also—are simply accessories, appurtenances to other persons' interests and purposes.[3]

The modular view of man and interpersonal relationships reduces man to little more than an object. The emphasis shifts from the value and dignity of men and women and places stress on their function. The Christian objects to any perspective which reduces the significance of man. He does so on grounds that man is made in God's image. In theory the objection may be clear enough, but practically speaking, is our approach to people wholistic? Do we know the people we worship with Sunday morning well enough to easily and genuinely pray with them? Are there divisions between our private home life, our religious church life, and our public work life? If you are a deacon or an elder, do you see your responsibility solely in terms of committee meetings and communion services, or do you see your fellow believers who are in need of spiritual nurture and discipline and physical provision? If our congregations

operate on an impersonal base, how will our approach to
the non-Christian be any different? A program orientation to
witnessing is in keeping with the mentality of our
modern age. It satisfies the believer in thinking that
something has been done, but does little in adding to the
body of believers. When the fragmented, impersonal
emphasis of modern human relationships is carried over
into the Christian perspective, the lostness of man
becomes an abstract and general phenomenon. It is a
faceless, abstract tragedy. We do not think of it in terms of
our neighbor, our family, our colleague.

The Gerasene demoniac may not fit your impression of
the modern man—progressive, contemporary, affluent,
and enlightened—but the rich young ruler, also described
in the Gospels, probably does. The young man, who
approached Jesus with the question, "Good Teacher, what
shall I do to obtain eternal life?" did not operate on the
relativistic standards of our own day. He knew the law, but
in a pride which parallels today's humanism; he believed
he had satisfied its demands. He stood before Jesus,
well-dressed and clear-thinking. The cultural gulf between
himself and the Gerasene demoniac could not have been
wider. He was all that the world respected while the
Gerasene demoniac was all that the world despised. Jesus'
words cut across anything that would have smacked of a
superficial programmed response to this young man. "One
thing you still lack; sell all that you possess and
distribute it to the poor, and you shall have treasure in
heaven; and come, follow Me" (Luke 18:22, NASB).
Nothing less than a total transformation was required. The
whole emphasis was away from what this man had done
and who this man was because of his wealth. The only
possible motivation available was a personal relationship
to Jesus Christ. Both he and the Gerasene demoniac stood
as whole men on the same spiritual level. Both required
redemption.

The Apostle Paul stated clearly that because of the life,
death, and resurrection of Jesus Christ "we recognize no
man according to the flesh" (2 Corinthians 5:16, NASB).
The modern mentality must not be allowed to cover up

man's spiritual need, nor dare we permit it to compromise our identity or distort a wholistic approach to people. The worldly standard of judging men must be eliminated. We must see humanity as Christ would have us see humanity—men and women for whom he died.

4

THE
ROMAN MILIEU:
THEN AS NOW

To be Christ's disciples in today's culture, we ought to have some understanding of how Christianity was manifested in the first century. We know that the Christian life has never existed in a cultural vacuum. There is constant tension between the way of the world and the way of Christ. Christ is still confronting and transforming culture now as he did then. Theoretically, the Christian acknowledges this, but actually he falls into two traps.

The first trap is a refusal to understand the Bible in its cultural and historical context. If all God meant for us to have was a collection of spiritual principles, he would not have given us the Bible. True spirituality has no meaning apart from the real world. Therefore, our study of God's Word is neither an academic nor devotional exercise designed to lift out the kernel of religious truth. God's Word not only declares the truth to us but models its application in a real-life situation. True Bible study means that we come to an understanding of the truth and its application. We are to be obedient to the historical precedent.

The second trap consists of knowing the truth, but not seeking by God's help to live in culture on the basis of truth. We may *know* all that the Bible says about the family and the use of our material goods, but when it comes right down to it, we *operate* according to culture's principles.

This two-pronged problem affecting our study of God's Word and our obedience to its truth can best be summarized in James's exhortation, "But prove yourselves doers of the word, and not merely hearers who delude themselves" (James 1:22, NASB). We may hear what the Word of God is saying, but we fail to apply the truth to our real-world situation. We have refused to think seriously and concretely of ways that the truth can be applied. Therefore, we are no longer "doers." This verse in James is a cliché to many of us and we readily nod our heads in agreement. Of course we should be "doers!" But the force of this challenge is not increased by the number of messages we hear on "be ye doers." The exhortation moves us only when we begin to act in obedience. A church that wrestles with carrying out God's Word in our modern culture is a church that knows the difference between merely hearing the Word and doing what the Word demands.

I am persuaded that one obstacle which hinders our understanding of God's Word and obedience to it in today's culture is a subtle conviction, among many, that there is a great disparity between the culture of the first century and the culture of the twentieth century. We readily admit that the nature of man has not changed; mankind will always need the gospel. But the cultural setting has been so transformed we feel we cannot implement the gospel in the same radical way. Only fishermen could just walk away from their trade and follow Christ. Only in an era free of corporate business could Christ demand that leaders be true servants, people who do not reflect in their ranking and salaries a superiority and higher privilege. Only in a society which did not rely on government aid could the church be commanded to care for the widow and orphan, to make provision for the elderly, and to feed the hungry.

Indeed there are tremendous differences between then and now, but the differences do not outweigh the similarities. The Roman milieu provided as pervasive a cultural context as our Western society. The complexities and tensions of that age rival our own day, making it no easier for the gospel to have taken root in the first century than it is for it to flourish in the twentieth century.

THE ROMAN CULTURE:
AN AGE OF COMPLEXITY AND TENSION

The Romans consolidated their military and diplomatic efforts under a strong unified rule. The empire was built to last. The hopes and desires of Caesar Augustus (30 B.C.-A.D. 14) were in some measure successful. Suetonius quotes from an edict issued by Augustus where he expresses his high goals, "May I be privileged to build firm and lasting foundations for the government of Rome." The prevailing influence of Hellenism, beginning with the conquests of Alexander the Great in the fourth century B.C., laid a cultural foundation upon which the Romans organized their empire. One of the most important factors to contribute to the unification of the empire was the development of Greek as the official language. The Romans went far beyond mere military occupation. Political organization, imperial citizenship, extensive taxation, transportation development by land and sea, and the Pax Romana all contributed to shaping people of diverse backgrounds into an empire.

Rostovtzeff characterized the empire as "a single economic unit. . . . knit together by the intensive exchange of all types of primary commodities and manufactured articles, including the four fundamental articles of trade: grain, wine, oil, and slaves."[1] Under Rome the rural economy came to an end. The legal and organizational abilities of the Romans were brought to bear in the formation of a world market. The upper middle class in Rome was responsible for the rise of commercial and financial companies. Never before had the world been so well suited for commerce with roads, the cross-cultural association, a common medium of communication, and commercial shipping. The very factors which made the empire great and in some respects more resistant to the gospel became instrumental in the advance of Christianity. The spirit of progressiveness, affluence, contemporaneity, and enlightenment of our own day must have been characteristic of the first century as well.

Geographically, the empire reached its greatest expanse under Trajan (A.D. 98-117) and its most productive economic activity under Antonines in the second century.[2] The Roman world of Christ's day was like a great ocean wave about to crest, sweeping humanity and history along in its power. The Rome of Augustus shaped the world far beyond his death in A.D. 14, but the birth of Christ, in approximately 6 B.C. in the little Judean town of Bethlehem, set in motion the fulfillment of God's eternal redemptive plan. Imbedded in the worldly Roman culture was the seed of God's kingdom. Do we realize how antagonistic to Christianity the morality, ethics, and mind-set of this pervasive cultural context were? Just to speak of the influence of the church upon culture would have been laughable to any Roman.

The external fabric of society was tightly knit by Rome's political organization and economic innovation. However, the internal structure of culture was torn by tension. The history of Roman emperors during this period is filled with intrigue, conspiracies, and assassinations. Augustus' successor, Tiberius, who reigned over the empire during Jesus' earthly ministry, was killed by Caligula, who reportedly smothered the bedridden Tiberius with the emperor's pillow. The people of Rome responded with delight, running through the city yelling, "To the Tiber with Tiberius!"—hardly a loyal response. Four years later, after Caligula had been assassinated by the palace guards, the people were more cautious. Suetonius explains why:

The terror inspired by Caligula's reign could be judged by the sequel; everyone was extremely reluctant to believe that he had really been assassinated, and suspected that the story was invented by himself to discover what people thought of him.[3]

The guards picked Claudius, who happened to be in the palace at the time of the murder, to be the next emperor.

His fourth wife, Agrippina, poisoned him after a thirteen-year reign and her seventeen-year-old son, Nero, came to power (A.D. 54). At thirty-two Nero ended his own life (A.D. 68), but not before nine years of tyrannical rule. Both Tacitus and Seutonius report that Nero blamed the Christians for the fire that swept through sections of Rome in A.D. 64. Tacitus writes,

But all human efforts, all the lavish gifts of the Emperor and the propitiation of the gods, did not banish the sinister belief that the conflagration was the result of an order (Nero's command). Consequently, to get rid of the report, Nero fastened the guilt and inflicted the most exquisite tortures on a class hated for their abominations, called Christians by the populace. . . . Mockery of every sort was added to their deaths. Covered with the skin of beasts, they were torn by dogs and perished, or were nailed to crosses or were doomed to the flames and burned to serve as nightly illumination, when daylight had expired. Nero offered his gardens for the spectacle, and was exhibiting a show in the circus, while he mingled with the people in the dress of a charioteer or stood aloft on a car.[4]

The cruelty of the emperors is equally matched by men in lesser positions of power. The fact that the Bethlehem massacre (Matthew 2) ordered by Herod the Great (37-4 B.C.) is not mentioned in any literature except the Bible does nothing to discredit the account. What were twenty-five babies or so to Herod? Herod is known to have killed his favorite wife, Marianime, her grandfather, her mother, his brother-in-law, and three of his sons, and during a swimming party at Jericho he drowned the high priest.[5]

Herod's son Antipas continued in his father's tradition, by beheading John the Baptist; his grandson, Agrippa I, was responsible for executing James, one of the twelve apostles (Acts 12:1-19). The turmoil of the age is apparent not only in the political leadership and the guerilla-style warfare between the Zealots and the Roman soldiers, but it is also evident in the numerous religions and philosophies that vied for men's allegiance. The impersonal and traditional state religions were used by the emperors

to instill within the populace a patriotic loyalty. In
contrast, the mystery religions emphasized man's
personal needs. These cults reflected the development of
animistic agricultural myths into individualistically
oriented urban religions. C. K. Barret comments,

*The myth, which seems often to have been cultically
represented, rested in many of these religions upon the
fundamental annual cycle of agricultural fertility; but
rites which probably were in earlier days intended to
secure productiveness in field and flock were now given
an individual application and effect.*[6]

Superficially some of the cults resembled Christianity.
The concepts of immortality and redemption were
important and were often symbolized in the secret
initiation rites. One of the most popular cults centered
around the mythological Persian god of light known as
Mithra. The cult taught that Mithra came to earth as a
warrior god and did meritorious deeds for mankind. The
ritual rites included both baptism and a meal at which the
initiates partook of bread, water, and wine.[7] Mithranism
sought to promote a high ethical standard, unlike many of
the cults, such as the cult of Atargatis from Syria, which
encouraged gross immorality. The first-century man easily
confused Christianity either with the mystery religions
or with Judaism. This placed pressure on the church to
clearly set forth the truth and to demonstrate its
uniqueness. F. F. Bruce summarizes,

*The pressure to recast Christianity as one among many
mystery religions was indeed so strong, albeit
unobtrusively so, that the wonder is not that there was
so much accommodation as there was but rather that the
original essence of Christianity as a faith and life based
not on a mystery drama, but on a historical person and
datable events, triumphed as it did. Whatever tendencies
to syncretism might appear, Christians continued to confess
Jesus as Lord in a unique sense, implying a Lordship
which could no more be shared with the lords of the
mystery cults than it could with the Roman emperor.*[8]

The believer must struggle to clarify the meaning of the gospel to a world confused by the variety of religious sentiments and numerous ecclesiastical bodies. But at the same time, the Christian can be encouraged that the Church of the first century waged an ongoing struggle against syncretism and accommodation. Like the Church today, they had traditions and thought-forms to contend with that threatened to subtly yet effectively eliminate the truth.

Like today's culture, the Roman world was to a great extent a "confederacy of cities."[9] The educational, economic, political, and religious life of the empire radiated from the cities. Rome was the ancient prototype of the twentieth-century urban center. The city faced many of the same problems our cities face today, such as unemployment, welfare doles, inadequate housing, and overpopulation. The "concrete jungle" of modern times apparently was evident in first-century Rome, for only the wealthy had enough land to enjoy a garden. F. R. Cowell comments on the housing situation:

The difficulty of providing housing for all the people who wanted to live in Rome forced the Romans before Imperial days to adopt the same sort of solution that prevails today in a city such as Paris or New York. Few except the rich could live in a town house or detached villa. The great majority were housed in blocks of tenements or apartments usually not more than three or four stories high. Early in the Empire, Augustus put a limit of 70 feet on the height of houses because of their rather shabby construction.[10]

If we were to walk the streets of Rome, we would witness the architectural monuments to the growth of secularism and paganism. The Public Treasury and the Forum were magnificent buildings, symbols of a new way in government, sophisticated and bureaucratic. The temples that lined these same streets encouraged a culturally accepted, state-supported paganism. The temples elevated rural animism to a position of prestige in the higher echelon of society and became a propaganda tool in the hand of the state. The mood of the Romans was reflected in the buildings they erected, just as our large shopping malls and dome stadiums indicate our interests. It was a city given over to a hedonistic life-style. In Paul's day there were three main theaters: Pompeii's theater with a seating capacity of 10,000, the theater of Balbus which held 8,000, and the theater of Marcellus which could seat 14,000. Besides these, there were the public baths, gymnasiums, and cruises.[11] But the gloss of great buildings and a thirst for entertainment does not tell us everything about the Romans. Seneca, one of the great Stoics of the time, expressed the despair he felt for the Roman citizen:

Consider this city [Rome] in which the throng that streams ceaselessly through its wildest streets is crushed to pieces whenever anything gets in the way to check its course as it streams like a rushing torrent, this city in which the seating space of three theatres is required at one time, in which is consumed all the produce of the plough from every land; consider how great would be the loneliness and the desolation of it if none should be left but those whom a strict judge would acquit.[12]

Seneca's description is almost as appropriate for a Western urbanite as it was for the Roman. But Rome was not the only urban center in the Empire. The New Testament gives insight into the culture of the day, especially through the ministry of Paul. Merrill Unger writes, "Paul's labors were confined to the centers of Graeco-Roman cultures and his strategy did not comprehend a dubious field. . . ."[13] Paul and Barnabas began their missionary efforts with a send off from the church at Antioch. Antioch was a commercial, racial, and political crossroads. F. F. Bruce writes, "By virtue of its land and sea communications it became an important commercial center. . . . Its cosmopolitan population and material wealth provided an apt setting for cultural exchange and religious syncretism."[14] It is in Antioch that the followers of Christ were first called "Christians." Can you imagine this small minority of believers penetrating a city of some 500,000 people, the third largest city in the Empire?[15] Antioch the Beautiful, as it was called, with its magnificent buildings and lamp-lighted streets and its pagan temples became the proving ground of the gospel. The cities that followed, such as Thessalonica, Pisidian Antioch, and Corinth, were significant commercial centers. Corinth especially was a hub of commercial activity. The city had two harbors separated by a ten-mile strip; one harbor received ships from the West and the other received ships from the East. The city's streets were crowded with merchants, soldiers, sailors, and tourists. The cult of Aphrodite, the goddess of love, exercised a dominating influence on the city. Merrill Unger estimates that more than a thousand prostitutes, religious priestesses of the cult, lived in luxurious quarters surrounding the temple on the Aeropolis.[16] Merrill Tenney writes, "Its sudden rise to wealth, its transient population, and the unlimited license which it afforded to all visitors made it a favorite resort for those who abandoned all restraint to their pleasures."[17]

Athens in Paul's day was an intellectual center. Its political and cultural influence had waned considerably. In many respects we might compare Athens to a contemporary university community. The Epicureans and the Stoics skeptically listened to Paul in the same quasi-tolerant, yet non-committed way that intellectualism looks down on Christianity today. The Athenian agora and the Areopagus (Mars Hill) were marks of an affluent, sophisticated, vain culture. It was in a city "full of idols" and intellectuals that Paul was provoked to speak (Acts 17), and although his message met with resistance and indifference, Luke tells us that some believed and gives us the names of two of them.

In contrast to Athens, the city of Ephesus reacted violently to the gospel. Success was greater there and so was the opposition. At the peak of the controversy the theater, which reportedly could hold 25,000, was filled with an angry mob shouting, "Great is Aretemis of the Ephesians!" At issue was the diminishing profits of Demetrius and other manufacturers of cult products who

stood to lose because of the gospel. Demetrius puts it
plainly:

*Men, you know that our prosperity depends upon this
business. And you see and hear that not only in Ephesus,
but in almost all of Asia, this Paul has persuaded and
turned away a considerable number of people, saying that
gods made with hands are no gods at all* [Acts 19:25, 26,
NASB].

In city after city we are impressed with a culture much
like our own. To be sure, substitutes have been found to
replace Aretemis or Aphrodite, but we still do have our
idols. Dare we ignore the tremendous cost required to truly
follow Christ in the first century? To those early
Christians it meant nothing at all simply to know of the
gospel theoretically. If the gospel was not applied, it was
not truly known and the person was not saved. We are wrong
if we think there is little real difference between our
culture and the way of Christ. Our culture is Corinthian in
its morality, Roman in its love for pleasure, Jewish in its
religiosity, Athenian in its intellectualism, and Ephesian in
its superstition. This is not to make these cities and
subcultures into mere caricatures of some modern-day
trends. The point is that the necessary distinctiveness of
the gospel in the first century is needed to be realized today
in the twentieth century. The question is not whether it
is more difficult to implement the commands of Christ
today than it was in the first century. Nor can 2,000 years
of Christianity fraught with failures and blessed with
successes be thrown up as an excuse. Christ confronted
culture then and he confronts culture now.

5.
THE TECHNOLOGICAL TOWER OF BABEL

The growth of the Church in the Roman world was not easily accomplished. Looking back on those days, we are quick to acknowledge the cultural factors that aided the advance of the gospel—such factors as a common language, transportation, and political and economic unity. But these advantages would have been useless if the Church had not lived up to its true identity. Apart from the supernatural work of God's Spirit and the commitment of Christ's followers, the Church would have soon disappeared into the cultural woodwork.

We live in a new day, but with similar pressures. We cannot afford to think that to live for Christ now is more difficult than it was to live for Christ then. Too many early Christians died rather than compromise their commitment to Christ. The modern age is dressed in an altogether different style, but the nature of man and his need has not changed. Paul's evaluation of man in Romans is as relevant today as ever. The truth of God is still exchanged for a lie, and the creature is still a victim of his own idolatry. The affluent, progressive, and enlightened modern man owns up to a world view clothed in the dress of the technological age.

It is an understatement to call our era, "The Scientific Age." Even if our pride in technology is slipping, we are the dependent children of manufactured conveniences and automation. Long ago we passed the threshold of invention. Today we find ourselves immersed in a technological whirlpool. The telephone, airplane, and computer were the harbingers of a new age. Scientific advance has become civilization's greatest concern and technological know-how has replaced our moral and spiritual reason.

Few of us despise the advantages technology has brought. If anything, the citizens of today's republic of technology have undervalued the benefits reaped from technology.[1] We have become familiar with the general accessibility of manufactured goods, temperature-controlled homes, cars, and shopping malls, and numerous household conveniences, to the point that it is hard to imagine any other kind of life. Because of technology, we live longer, work less, and generally are better educated than our ancestors. However, appreciating the benefits of technology is one thing. Recognizing technology's domination is quite another. I do not mean by "domination" our seemingly inseparable attachment to the automobile, television, and telephone. If we had to, we could even live without these "necessities." But technology's impact is far greater. It shapes and expresses the world view of modern man. The benefits have not been accepted at face value, but instead, have been turned into symbols of man's independence from God. Automation does not simply mean the manufacturing of goods. It represents the indistinguishable union of man and machine. Computers are much more than a valuable storehouse for necessary information. They are seen as the mediating means to make the present-day impossibilities future necessities.

Technology is the instrument by which modern man works out his philosophy of life. Will Herberg, a distinguished Jewish sociologist, has written,

Human problems are increasingly seen as technological problems to be dealt with by adjustments and manipulation. . . . In fact the belief seems to have

emerged that there is nothing beyond man's desires, nothing beyond man's power. His values are his to make or unmake.[2]

Operating on the basis of a "Tower of Babel" mentality, modern man pushes on, irrespective of the commands of his Creator. His only boundary is the illusion of his limitless potential. He has no creed but the "survival of the fittest."

We have taken such elaborate precautions to provide ideal climatic conditions that we no longer experience our natural climate. We shop in huge air-conditioned shopping malls, watch sports in domed stadiums or in the comfort of our living rooms, and fly from Chicago to San Francisco 35,000 feet over deserts and mountains in a temperature-controlled cabin. "Our roots," writes Daniel Boorstin, "grow in an antiseptic hydroponic solution. Instead of enjoying the weather given us 'by Nature and by Nature's God' (in Jefferson's phrase) we worry about the humidifier and the air-conditioner."[3] Boorstin's point is well taken. Many today are up in arms not only because technology has created an artificial environment, but because they believe technology threatens the very *survival* of the environment. Both the "romantic" and the environmentalist are calling for an end to technological exploitation.

Not all Christians agree on how to handle the environment. One may demonstrate against the construction of a nuclear power plant out of the conviction that it poses a potential danger to man and his environment. Another believer, considering the plant safe, may support its construction in order to meet energy needs. Disagreement over specific environmental matters is bound to occur, but all Christians should share a genuine concern for God's creation. The earth is not a theatrical stage upon which man plays out his existence. The earth is as much a part of creation as man is. Its beauty, resources, and power reveal some of the attributes of Almighty God.

Boorstin makes an additional point. Not only does technology tend to "immunize" us from our "raw landscape" but technology "isolates" us from one another. Technology has served to promote the functional efficiency of man. Computers, assembly lines, and 747s have sped up communications, production, and transportation but they have not enhanced the personal-relational qualities of men and women. Correspondence has been reduced to computer read-outs and the work place to an assembly line. A sales representative will fly half-way around the world to see a client without conversing with his seatmate because they are both listening to recorded music through earphones.[4]

Technology expresses what is inherent in modern man's spiritual condition. Technology did not invent pollution or generate individualism. Separation between man and his environment and between man and other men is a result of the Fall. Boorstin fails to make the most important observation. Technology creates an artificial spiritual environment where man believes he is insulated from and independent of the Lord of the universe. More often than not, it is man's failures, not his successes, that make him think of God. Economic strength, industrial growth, scientific discovery, major advances in medicine, and space exploration are not likely to make men think of God. Wars and disasters may harden men against God, but technological success causes men to ignore God.

For even though they knew God, they did not honor Him as God, or give thanks; but they became futile in their speculations, and their foolish heart was darkened [Romans 1:21, NASB].

It is difficult to imagine any first-century Roman citizen judging the thoughts of an engineer or scientist or industrialist as "futile" and "foolish." After all, we would expect even our great grandfathers to be amazed at the progress we have made. Would the Apostle Paul be impressed if he were to visit our laboratories and launching pads and don safety glasses and walk along the assembly line? As he talked to the line foreman, the lab technician, and the researcher, would Paul have been convinced that modern man worshiped his Creator and obeyed the revelation of his Word? I believe the answer is obvious. What Paul wrote to the Roman church, he would have to write today to believers in New York, Tokyo, or Sao Paulo. The wisdom and productivity of our technological progress stands in sharp contrast to modern man's ignorance of God.

Even the popular reaction against the domination of technology fails to acknowledge the Creator. There seems to be room in today's speculation for agnosticism, atheism, and mysticism, but no room for the Lord of the universe. Man's own creativity has intensified his despair. It is increasingly apparent that man has not found himself in the technological breakthroughs of the twentieth century.

In the history of man, the Tower of Babel is as contemporary as it is ancient. The primitive call to technology was first echoed in the cradle of civilization. "Come, let us make bricks, and burn them thoroughly" (Genesis 11:3, NASB). The sun-dried bricks of clay were replaced by bricks baked with intense heat, making them as hard as stone. These newly invented bricks were held in place by asphalt, a resource which abounded in the area around Babylon. With these new construction materials, the people of Shinar were able to build durable, multi-storied buildings. Their new technique may not seem very impressive today, but it was then. By experimenting with asphalt as mortar material, they discovered a valuable natural resource. They improved their living conditions by building bigger and better homes. "Better homes make better living" and similar real estate slogans may not be so contemporary.

There was nothing wrong with Shinar's inhabitants desiring progress and cultural advance. Their call to technology, "Come, let us make bricks, and burn them thoroughly" was perfectly legitimate and reflected their ingenuity. However, the people went beyond the benefits of their technology and used their new-found technique to express their oneness with the technological age. These primitive moderns followed up their call to technology with a philosophy of life.

Come, let us build for ourselves a city, and a tower whose top will reach into heaven, and let us make for ourselves a name; *lest we be scattered abroad over the face of the whole earth* [Genesis 11:4, NASB].

This brief summary of their world view captures the modern sentiment. Their motivation was fundamentally that of fear. "Let us build . . . lest we be scattered abroad." They envisioned their security in unity and their strength in human solidarity. Making a name for themselves should not be interpreted as a casual desire for recognition. They were out to create a physical and spiritual monument which would inspire confidence and assure their independence. Jacques Ellul writes,

To make a name for oneself has nothing to do with the modern expression referring to a reputation; it means to become independent, and that is what their attempt at building meant. The people wanted to be definitely separated from God. . . . It is the desire to exclude God from his creation. And it is this solidarity in a name, this unity in separation from God, which was to keep men from ever again being separated on earth.[5]

The people of Shinar ought to remind us of the behavioralist or materialist today who sees all of life from only the empirical dimension. To these people, the complexity of man's moral and spiritual nature is ultimately reducible to chemical reactions and environmental conditions. Even these primitive moderns found it intellectually comforting to reduce their problem and the solution to the flatland of humanism. Not one word is explicitly stated either for or against God in their world view. They took for granted their origin and their abilities and accepted without question their capacity for technology. Fearful of alienation and the unknown vastness of "the face of the whole earth," they did exactly what modern man does. They evaluated their situation from a naturalistic perspective and ended up eliminating their moral and spiritual responsibilities before God.

Are we not fearful today of inner emptiness and loneliness? Do we have sufficient ground for personal value and the dignity of man in the face of the seemingly limitless frontiers both of the cosmos and the microcosmos? The unknown is all around us.

The early inhabitants of civilization were optimistic. Their discovery gave them incentive to solve their problem. After all, given sufficient time, adequate resources, and human intelligence, what difficulty could not be solved? Technology gave these people hope. They anticipated success as they baked the bricks and set them in the asphalt mortar. More than likely, all other considerations became secondary. Their number-one concern was the daily construction of the Tower of Babel.

It is strange that we should find an example of ourselves so early in human history. Like modern man, their lives were filled with paradox. They knew both fear and hope. They were proud of their technological intelligence and yet were indifferent toward God. They took courage from outward unity, but experienced inner loneliness. Surrounding themselves with the truths of their own creation, they pushed their plaguing doubts into dark corners. The Tower of Babel mentality may have diluted personal differences and leveled personal conviction to one common denominator, but it did not eliminate their God-given moral and spiritual dimension. The seeds of dissatisfaction are permanently rooted in fallen man. Despair is the emerging impulse of every world view that excludes the centrality of Jesus Christ.

And the Lord came down to see the city and the tower which the sons of men had built. And the Lord said, "Behold they are one people, and they all have the same language. And this is what they began to do, and now nothing which they purpose to do will be impossible for them. Come, let Us go down and there confuse their language, that they may not understand one another's speech" [Genesis 11:5-7, NASB].

There is no question that the people were successful. They had engineered a truly impressive city. God indicated as much when he said, "Nothing which they purpose to do will be impossible for them." However, the meaning of that statement must be understood. To the ears of modern man it sounds more like a commendation than a judgment. Was God jealous of man's success? From all outward signs here was man at his best; creative, industrious, and accomplished.

In an age of unarrested technological momentum, it is probably impossible to convince twentieth-century man that God judged Babel out of mercy. We would like nothing better than the self-assurance that whatever we purpose to do we will do. Complete and unrestrained technological advance would undoubtedly ensure modern man's security. Or would it? We are almost as successful today as the early inhabitants of Babel; successful enough to realize from God's perspective why he found it necessary to break up their solidarity. As it throws ethics aside and screens out the moral issue, technology becomes utilitarian. If something can be done, it will be done. Alvin Toffler comments,

Despite profound ethical questions about whether they should, the fact remains that scientific curiosity is, itself, one of the most powerful driving forces in our society. In the words of Dr. Rollin D. Hotchkiss of the Rockefeller Institute: "Many of us feel instinctive revulsion at the hazards of meddling with the finely balanced and far-reaching systems that make an individual what he is. Yet I believe it will surely be done or attempted. The pathway will be built from a combination of altruism, private profit, and ignorance."[6]

The symbols of a mechanistic and materialistic world view are as terrifying as they are appealing. The nuclear age is a relativistic age with overwhelming paradoxes. Man has invented weapons of unimaginable destruction and at the same time invented life-saving drugs. Scientists can produce an atomic explosion by bringing together two radioactive uranium piles, or they can place cobalt between two radioactive uranium piles and produce cobalt-60, a material widely used in killing human cancer cells. Many hospitals are equipped with highly specialized, professionally staffed pediatric intensive care units. The survival chances for premature or sick babies has greatly improved. But at the same time, doctors abort literally thousands of babies annually. Only the whim of the mother stands between science's ability to use every means at its disposal to ensure survival and the brutal yet routine abortion. No other civilization has experienced the intensity and comprehensiveness of modern communication. Yet modern art, literature, and movies are permeated with an overwhelming sense of alienation and meaninglessness. We are gifted with such an array of conveniences and possessions that it is almost impossible to imagine human existence apart from them. We are possessed by technology's invented needs. According to Boorstin, "We will be misled if we think that technology will be directed primarily to satisfying 'demands' or 'needs' or to solving recognized 'problems'. . . . Technology is a way of multiplying the unnecessary."[7] Technology has not only freed man to study himself, but it has opened new frontiers of scientific research. Man's behavior has become one of our popular fascinations. Fed by the incessant research of psychology, psychiatry, and sociology, computer banks are brimming with collected data on every facet of the human specimen. Never has man been more predictable and never has he been more manipulated. The more we know of man the less we are able to treat men like men. The call to technology and its accompanying philosophy of life has led to the depersonalization of man. The individual is lost in the will of the masses, pushed along by an irreversible momentum.

Dr. Walter R. Hearn relates the following experience which occurred to him after the purchase of an analytical instrument necessary for the completion of his research project.

After the instrument was delivered, I spent a week at the manufacturer's training course for operators of the instrument, with perhaps thirty other people from around the country. Something about that week got to me. The instrument at that time cost about $14,000. Inflation and increased sophistication have pushed the price up to $18,000 or $20,000 by now [1973]. It occurred to me that

*each of the thirty people in the class was of infinitely more
worth than that, but we did not come together to learn
how to draw the best out of each other. We were there to
focus on this machine because it was worth $14,000 and
we were obligated to treat it well and maximize its great
potential.*

*I tried to get to know some of my classmates, but it was
difficult. They were intent on their responsibility to master
the instrument, and at the end of each day they rushed to
anesthetize themselves at the free bar provided by the
manufacturer. They could not stand the company of the
machine without the palliative effect of alcohol, but not
the company of other human beings. . . .*

*In science, as in other fields, the machines we have
increasingly come to rely on are highly complex,
"almost human." But as machines take on more human
attributes, we see human beings not freed to become
more human, as we had hoped, but constrained to become
more and more like machines. This mechanization of
people seems to come not so much from understanding
ourselves mechanistically as from competing among
ourselves for the available resources.* [8]

Toffler captures the feeling of many when he writes,

*More and more, there is a growing weariness and wariness,
a pall of pessimism, a decline in our sense of mastery.
More and more, the environment comes to seem chaotic,
beyond human control.* [9]

Although our faith in technology is slipping and warnings
can be heard from many quarters, very little can be done
to impede the momentum of our modern Tower of Babel
mentality. Human solidarity can be measured by the
escalating cultural consensus against God and his revealed
absolutes. At a time when many in the West are raising
doubts as to the superiority of technological solutions, the
passion of other nations to be full-fledged members of
the technological age is overwhelming. The Tower of Babel
mentality transcends ideological differences and national
boundaries. It makes little difference whether one is a

capitalist or communist if he shares the same united front against God.

So the Lord scattered them abroad from there over the face of the whole earth; and they stopped building the city [Gen. 11:8, NASB].

The insulated, artificial spiritual environment was destroyed. In spite of their success, the fears of these primitive moderns came true. God confused their language and they were scattered over the face of the earth. God did not destroy the Tower! But he reversed its symbol. It no longer represented man's united commitment to a manmade ideology. Instead it marked the place where chaos reigned because of man's disobedience and God's judgment. Man was brought face to face with the realities of his dilemma and the wickedness of his plastic culture. The native etymology for Babylon is "Bab IL" which means "The gate of God." The Hebrews interpreted Babel quite differently. For them it meant "confusion."[10]

Down through the ages we hear the Babylonians declare, "We are the gate to God" and the Bible counters, "No, you are confusion." Throughout the Word of God, Babylon symbolizes a great and mighty civilization turned away from God.

The twentieth-century believer lives in just such a civilization. Technology in itself is not wrong. As descendants of Adam, we are subject to God's creation mandate. Nature not only can be known, it should be known. Man is given the inexhaustible challenge to "rule over" and "subdue" the whole earth. The Fall of man did not remove God's mandate but it did change man's enjoyable, positive, and constructive task into a fight for survival. Fear and superstition came to dominate man's thoughts. It was not until men of spiritual conviction began to explore creation that the door to modern science and technology was opened. Many of these men were not only the fathers of modern science, but they were also students of the Bible.[11] Their conviction in God both as the Creator and the Redeemer spurred them on to discover new truths, formulate fundamental principles, and establish experimental procedures. Galileo, Faraday, and Kepler believed that nature was "shot through with rationality." Isaac Newton, James Maxwell, and Robert Boyle understood their scientific labors as an exercise of stewardship. These scientists were convinced that the order, wonder, and power of creation was established and sustained by an all-knowing, all-powerful God. Their research was not divorced from their worship.[12]

We have come a long way since those early years of scientific discovery. The world view which stimulated modern research is now either ignored or despised. The responsibilities of a steward have been exchanged for the ascendancy of a master. Today's materialism, depersonalization, and moral relativism are not merely the negative side effects of technological success. They are part and parcel of a way of life which operates as if God did not exist.

Is it right for the Church of Jesus Christ to huddle in the shadows of the technological Tower of Babel? Is it right for believers to sell their stewardship for the small conveniences of social and intellectual conformity? Is it right that evangelicals are swept along by the same impulses and drives as the builders of the Tower?

It is into this world that Jesus Christ sends us, not to conform but to be transformed. We are not lab technicians and assembly line workers who just happen to be Christians. We are not television producers, lawyers, and house-painters who happen to have their religious convictions down pat. We are Christian scientists, Christian businessmen, and Christian clerks. Men and women who are in the process of being shaped by the Word and Spirit of God. "Low-profile" Christianity has no place in the spiritually helpless, decadent twentieth century. Far too much is at stake for Christians to live with shallow convictions and worldly indifference. Whether or not Jesus Christ appears as the Son of God to members of the technological age depends upon our faithfulness to his truth, to his sacrificial love, and to the expectation of his second coming. Primarily, our motivation is not to change the system. It is to be changed by Christ in the system.

We act then, on faith—not with the certain knowledge that our deeds will alter history's course, but with the inner assurance that holding forth such a faith is the first and most important act required of us. [13]

6
THE MEDIA

The mass media reflect our culture. They transmit the twentieth-century ethos of Western society. Values, morals, behavioral models, and material expectations are portrayed incessantly through media which challenge no self-evaluation or real outside opposition. If we were to hear a lecturer affirm immorality as a constructive way of life, and affluence as the goal of each North American, we would immediately object and feel compelled to refute his position. The media are not as direct as the lecturer, but far more powerful. No men, no matter how charismatic or powerful, have ever held a greater grip on culture than have the modern media. The media are the modern manipulators of our collective consciousness, leveling man to a depersonalized mass. How we think, act, learn, and communicate is greatly controlled by the media, making them not only reflectors of culture, but creators of culture. Through their influence we are evaluated, conditioned, and appealed to, and in the process, made subject to the commercialism and escapism of the twentieth century. In an article entitled, "The Scary World of T.V.'s Heavy Viewer" George Gerbner writes,

Never before have such large and varied publics—from the nursery to the nursing home, from ghetto tenement to penthouse—shared so much of the same cultural system of

messages and images, and the assumptions embedded in them. Television offers a universal curriculum that everyone can learn.[1]

Marshall McLuhan's well-known idea, "the medium is the message," suggests that the media say something about our culture over and above the content of the "tube." The mass media are both reflective and manipulative of our culture. They are impersonal, oriented toward action, vicarious, amoral, and commercial.

THE MEDIA ARE IMPERSONAL

The viewer and the performer are brought together through the media. We see people and places that we never would have seen without the media. We know more people and are exposed to more information than our forefathers could have dreamed of. Neil Harris writes in a *Time* essay, "We absorb a quantity of information each day that could have sated our ancestors for a year or more."[2] We are brought together via TV with the leaders of the world and our folk heros; the celebrities and the athletes. We are witnesses to congressional hearings, bedroom scenes, and riots. But this exposure also means isolation. The media transmit a visible image with an invisible barrier. While creating "bigger than life personalities," television distorts what it seeks to represent and catapults its subjects into a fantasy-like fame. Camera and screen form a wall between the televised subject and the viewing masses. The isolation, however, is far deeper than between the TV personality and the 40 million faithful viewers. There is an anonymity about television and the movies that the public finds comforting. We can sit for hours engaged but not involved. Television becomes a release—exactly what we need or think we need after a routine day at work or school. Television does not demand our involvement. It is strictly a spectator's hobby. Our inexhaustible hunger for the news is fed by a massive network of men and technological machines, but the intensive exposure results in apathy as much as it does action. We have become immune to what we see. We are put on the scene of wars and famines while remaining within the safety and security of our living rooms. The only viewer response that the televison industry is really concerned about is the sale of advertized products. We have tuned in in order to turn off.

THE MEDIA ARE ACTION-ORIENTED

Although the viewer is kept inactive, the programming depends on a steady stream of action. Robin Day, a prominent British TV commentator writes, "For television journalism this means a dangerous and increasing concentration on action (usually violent and bloody) rather than on thought, on happenings rather than issues, on shock rather than explanation, on personalities rather than ideas."[3] Much of what the viewer sees is "designed action." The viewer's attention is played for by every means available. This is especially noticeable in the commercials. Alvin Toffler comments, "In an effort to transmit even richer image-producing messages at an even faster rate, communications people, artists, and others consciously work to make each instant of exposure to the mass media carry a heavier informational and emotional freight."[4]

Violence is a different form of action, but its purpose is much the same; namely, to keep the viewer's interest. Edwin Kiesler Jr., in an article entitled, "T.V. Violence: What Can Parents Do?" says, "Your child, if he's typical, will watch 13,000 people die on television before he is 15 years old. If he were to see every show on network prime time this year, he would witness murders, beatings, rape, muggings, and robberies at the rate of eight an hour, with three out of four programs featuring violence."[5] The impression of violence is etched in the viewer's mind, but the reality of violence remains vague. In real life such violence would sicken us, but watching it on TV we are absorbed in the drama. What is the impact of TV violence on us? George Gerbner and Larry Gross conclude that the "acceptance of violence and passivity in the face of injustice may be consequences of far greater social

concern than occasional displays of individual aggression."[6]
Few of us believe that TV violence will rub off on our own
behavior. However, that line of defense may be veiling
television's more subtle impact. Dr. David Pearl, Chief of
the Behavioral Sciences Research Branch National Institute
of Mental Health says,

*It's always someone else whose emotional health is
endangered by a diet of violence. It's the kids, or the guy
next door, or the people in some social environment other
than one's own. We are always sure violent material is
bad for everybody else, but we're adult enough to handle
it.*[7]

Whether we care to admit it or not, we suffer from a
steady diet of violent acts. The narrow range of legitimate
violence needed to portray the fullness of true drama has
ballooned out of proportion, serving as the cheapest
means both in dollars and talent to keep the viewer's
attention. The impact of the media's bent toward action
may leave us passive to the complex needs and problems
which confront us from outside the media-world of
personalities and one-hour solutions.

It also limits the content of communication. We are
conditioned to listen to only those messages clothed in the
media's action-packed style. Careful, rational thought
becomes a secondary requirement. One is absorbed into the
message in order to understand the message. It is
increasingly more difficult to speak to twentieth-century
man, simply because he is bored by the thought
processes inherent in meaningful communication. This is
true for the non-Christian who refuses to contemplate his
own spiritual need and to seek for a solution, not because
he is repulsed by such things, but because he is bored by
them.

The Christian is also affected. It is much easier to
follow a TV plot than to study God's Word and apply its
teaching. Thinking bores us while watching TV excites
us. For many there is no comparison between the time spent
in Bible study and the time spent watching TV. The
shallowness of modern man and the superficiality of many

believers stems in part from an over-exposure to one form of communication. This form has the undesirable effect of making human contemplation mundane and person-to-person communication on any subject of real consequence tedious.

THE MEDIA ARE VICARIOUS

The media are substitutes for human experience. Many live their lives through the people they see on the screen. Real communication is replaced by watching two celebrities reading a script, and physical activity is substituted by watching others at work, play, and in sports. Our desire to lead challenging and creative lives is met vicariously through the media. Naturally, we tend to model our behavior after TV personalities. Alvin Toffler writes,

These vicarious people, both live and fictional, play a significant role in our lives, providing models for behavior, acting out for us vicarious roles and situations from which we draw conclusions about our own lives.[8]

The world is not able to absorb the transient, illusory world of TV and still maintain stability. The turmoil people feel in living vicarious lives, with a gulf between the media world they enjoy and a real world they are indifferent to, is reflected by the people instrumental in shaping television. The trauma of learning to cope with day-to-day life in a world not manipulated by the camera or cut and spliced in an editing room is felt most keenly by television's stars. The instability they personally experience is passed on to thousands of people who grope for appropriate images to emulate and behavioral norms to follow.

The vicarious world of television is a confusing world. Neil Harris observes,

On television in particular, dramatized commercials, world calamities and local anecdotes are presented in astonishing juxtaposition without apparent effort at assigning priorities.[9]

The media do not demand commitment or decision. They fail to distinguish between the varied needs and responsibilities of men: both the important and the unimportant are repeated over and over, from the silliest commercial to the President's news conference. People are conditioned to expect the instant replay. Harris observes the impact of the "second chance opportunity".

Because information can be so easily repeated, neither concentration nor memory is critical to its absorption; at times they even interfere with the pleasure of reception. The instant replay is based on this principle of the second chance, a world without necessities that can transcend any barrier. The new stadium in New Orleans houses giant television screens, assuring spectators of the same opportunity to re-examine exciting moments that they would have had in their living rooms. [10]

Apart from eating, sleeping, and working, television has become for many one of the most important elements in life. Our daily routine of living often is carefully organized to ensure availability for all our favorite programs.

THE MEDIA ARE AMORAL

Judging from a biblical point of view, we may be inclined to say that much of what we see in the media advocates an immoral life-style. However, the media attempt to project a position of neutrality on moral issues, and have sought to remove the question of morality from the mind of the viewer. The trivial, superficial plot of a two-hour movie is laden with very critical moral and ethical issues. A couple may lie, steal, and fornicate, yet the viewer is absorbed in a story plot which he has seen numerous times before in similar shows. The sexual explicitness of some movies forces the issue to the forefront. But TV's subtle form of indoctrination is by far more pervasive and effective. Both the "good" and the "bad" think nothing of free sex. Sexual morality is represented as an issue of the past; one which contemporary man has outgrown. The supposed tolerance of the media in this area raises the serious question of civilization's survival. If the number-one curriculum for modern man's education refuses to distinguish between what is sexually moral and immoral, then we have nothing to expect but emotionally scarred, physically sick young people and fragmented families. The distinguished anthropologist, J. D. Unwin observes,

Any human society is free to choose either to display great energy or to enjoy sexual freedom. The evidence is that it cannot do both for more than one generation. [11]

THE MEDIA ARE COMMERCIAL

Robert Hargreaves comments,

Television in America dedicates itself wholly and solely to the principles of commercialism. To understand that, is the first step toward understanding television as it is presently constituted in the United States. [12]

Television's product is people. A program director promises to deliver to a sponsor a certain number of people. The profit-motive is the sole determining factor. People are seen as a commodity purchasable by the sponsor. The most sought after and appealed to segments of culture are the young and middle aged. Programs are designed to hold the viewer through the entire evening. It is not just the ads, but the programming itself which is geared to commercial interests. The *New Yorker* magazine reports, "All have achieved complete homogenization of comedy, drama, variety, news, sports, public affairs, that will produce exactly the same mild tangy taste."[13] The leveling of programming to the lowest common denominator for the largest number of people assures the industry of the greatest profits. The profits for 1976, on a gross of six billion, will be close to a billion dollars. Kenneth Curtis comments,

. . . broadcasters will claim they are chiefly devoted to using the public airwaves for our best interests, but the overriding criterion of profit actually informs all decisions

*and policies. Any broadcasting executive who lapses in
his grasp of this reality is easily and quickly replaced, for
the stakes are high.* [14]

The television industry is on a profit-making par with North
America's major companies. The TV may serve as priest,
teacher, and entertainer, but first and foremost, it is a
merchant, in the big business of selling the world on a
lifestyle. After two years of doctoral research into
commercials, Kenneth Curtis concluded that they
"represent an insidious assault on the Christian view of
life." He writes,

*Jesus taught us that our life does not consist of the
abundance of things possessed. The commercials, when
taken as a whole and seen cumulatively, reply that one's
life consists precisely in the abundance of things we
possess.* [15]

Curtis goes on to point out that the Christian's life-style
has always been in conflict with the way of the world.
Conformity to the world in any age is sin, but in our own
day the pressures to conform have been intensified through
the media. Two questions arise out of this discussion on
the nature of the media. If the media are impersonal,
action-oriented, vicarious, amoral, and commercial, how
is the Christian to live with their influence? Second, to what
extent have the modern media affected the proclamation of
the gospel?

As we have seen from personal experience, television
exerts a tremendous influence in many areas of culture,
including interpersonal relationships, family life,
education, social behavior, the manner and content of
communication, and materialism. The Christian must
work out several important steps.

1. The believer must be educated to the nature and
function of the media. He must recognize the media as
agents of this world. They are tools used both to reflect as
well as to create the modern culture. Therefore, their impact
must be studied and analyzed. Manipulation is prevented
by a conscious awareness of the central motives of our

culture and a deepening appreciation for the Word of God. The Christian has, in his fellowship with God and fellow believers, an authentic counterpart to the dehumanization-depersonalization of the mass media.

2. The believer must discipline his exposure to the media. A great deal of our TV-watching and movie-going is done out of habit. We fill up our free time with television, without considering the variety of constructive alternatives available to us. The good TV programs can be better enjoyed without watching hours of mediocre and poor programming, and there is a great deal of television that the Christian should do without. To have no discretion over viewing habits is sinful. Besides being a waste of time, excessive TV exposure produces a harmful mental input. Television is an important part of our culture. The Christian ought to be mindful of its impact and wise in its use.

3. The believer must develop a sensitivity to a media-conditioned culture. It is important to understand the nature of the media and to regulate one's own viewing habits, but in addition, we must authenticate our own communication. Individuals in the world will not be encouraged to turn to Christ if the gospel is communicated in the same way the media transmit the spirit of our age. This brings us to a second question. To what extent have the electronic media, especially television, proclaimed the gospel?

Some time ago, Joe Bayly wrote a book entitled *The Gospel Blimp*. It was a satiric look at some inappropriate methods of mass evangelism.[16] The plot revolved around a group of men in a typical middle-class suburb who got the bright idea they would witness to their neighbors by dropping evangelistic tracts from a blimp. Their plan backfired and little was accomplished except to waste their energy and antagonize their neighbors. The *Blimp* method represents an approach which seeks to dissimulate the gospel in some impersonal manner calling for a superficial decision and failing to convince the hearers of anything more than an egocentric gospel. Evangelism without the media can be just as cold and impersonal and ineffective as with the media. But there is no doubt that the media intensify the flaws and shallowness of our approach. Call-in talk shows, media blitzes, and television teasers are nothing more than gimmicks, and when they are used to proclaim the gospel, the Church is at its cheapest. What Robert Hargreaves writes about television in general is applicable to a great deal of so-called Christian broadcasting.

With the honorable exception of the news broadcasts, the fare is universally bland, unexciting, and excessively timid. Controversy is generally shunned, issues avoided, self-censorship commonplace. Anything that might cause the audience to think is expressly, and by fiat, forbidden. [17]

When there is flagrant misuse of the media by Christians it would be better if the media were not used at all. In such a case, nothing can be achieved except the loss of money given by God's people, and a serious distortion of the gospel. Such broadcasting designs its programming to satisfy the nominal Christian constituency. By appealing to the "lowest common denominator" they are assured of enough popularity to produce a steady money flow, but few individuals are actually added to a local body of believers. A proper use of the media must first transform the nature and function of the media as expressed above.

Instead of a dehumanizing, impersonal approach we must be prepared to speak to people as individuals in need of God's redemptive love. A personal approach does not mean reading people's names on the air or praying for them by name. It does mean speaking to men's hearts and minds, replacing the shallow, action-oriented message and attention teasers with the true gospel, a message content which will challenge and offend. It will cause some to turn their televisions off and others to listen attentively.

An appeal to men's minds and a church-oriented follow-up are necessary for a personal approach to individuals. When the viewer remains a spectator, responding passively to the gospel, nothing is achieved. Emphasis on appropriating the gospel and joining with other believers will dissuade the viewer from settling for a vicarious experience that ends when the program does.

Anything that is suggestive of commercial interest or technique must be eliminated. Evangelism is to be characterized by self-sacrifice. Raising support on the air may continue the program, but it distorts the gospel.

The wise use of the media calls for men and women of God committed to an authentic communication of the gospel. Those with technical skills, creativity, and spiritual depth are needed to produce programs, and others in the body of believers are needed to give of their time and energy in follow-up and financial assistance.

Jacques Ellul offers a perspective that we ought to bear in mind, even if we do not agree with it entirely.

...we are living in a society which is no longer based on direct personal relationships, but on media and on distant and complex collective Interests. ... How can we manage to incorporate that into Christianity? How can we think of Christianity in terms of this factual situation? [I contend that this is a false situation] ... It is a question natural to the intellect of man, but false in as far as it falsifies revelation. Every act of love shown in Scripture involves causing a person to come out of his status of anonymity, derived from collectivity, the crowd, etc. in order, through a purely personal relationship, to transform him into a person known and distinguished by his name. Love, biblically, is never turned into something for media, nor is it collectivized, abstract or general. ... Technological means and population increase can create mechanized communities of interest, doing away with personal encounter through the multiplicity of external contacts and through the formation of "the solitary crowd."[18]

JESUS THE COMMUNICATOR

Earlier we saw that Jesus spoke to the whole man. He cut through the cultural barriers. There could be no neutrality in the fact of his redemptive Word and his clear

command, "Follow me." One instance which especially
stands out as an indication of Jesus' communication to
the "masses" was the feeding of the 5,000. Read the sixth
chapter of John and you will see several stages of
communication. The first stage was the miraculous
provision of food. Jesus did not see a faceless mass of
humanity; he saw people in need of food. We should not
take for granted his perception of the need nor the fact
that he felt responsible to do something about it. There is
nothing here which suggests that Jesus simply used the
occasion to reveal his identity as the Son of God. Providing
food was not a mere good-will gesture, it was an essential
part of authentic, evangelistic communication. I do not
believe we can equate this mass provision of food with a
showy song number by a Christian quartet on television.
The music group may get people's attention and fulfill
the audience's entertainment needs, but it does not
demonstrate as Jesus did, the compassion and the
capacity to provide for man's fundamental needs. Jesus
used this opportunity to impress upon his disciples the
importance of providing men's needs. He asked Philip how
to meet the need in order to test him, and he used the
disciples to distribute the food.

The first stage of communication was not without
problems. The people misconstrued this provision of food as
an end in itself. They were eager to secure their own
physical well-being by establishing Jesus as their leader.
Jesus heard the "feedback" and responded accordingly.

*Jesus therefore perceiving that they were intending to
come and take Him by force, to make Him king,
withdrew again to the mountain by Himself alone* [John
6:15, NASB].

No opportunity was given for the rise of a personality cult.
Having met their need and frustrated their attempt to
manipulate his message, Jesus proceeded to the second
stage of communication.

The multitude followed Jesus to Capernaum. They were
intrigued, interested, and ready for an explanation. The
explanation that followed was not what they had in mind.

Jesus spoke of a relationship between his miraculous provision of food and their spiritual need.

Do not work for the food which perishes, but for the food which endures to eternal life, which the Son of Man shall give to you, for on Him the Father, even God, has set His seal [John 6:27, NASB].

His message was unambiguous and uncompromising. It forced his listeners to think, to grapple with an issue far more profound than where their next meal was coming from. Jesus' words, "I am the Bread of Life," intensified the communication. They had to deal with Jesus on a different level than they had anticipated. Jesus was not indifferent to their reception of the gospel, but neither did he deny the necessary power of God to convict and lead men to the truth: "All that the Father gives Me shall come to Me."

The second stage ends with negative feedback. The Jews understood his message, but doubted its truthfulness. By that time the majority must have been waning in their interest. A political leader and a physical provider they could follow, but not someone who claimed to meet men's spiritual needs.

In the third stage of communication Jesus reiterates his message and further intensifies it.

Truly, truly, I say to you, unless you eat the flesh of the Son of Man and drink His blood, you have no life in yourselves. He who eats My flesh and drinks My blood has eternal life; and I will raise him up on the last day. For My flesh is true food, and My blood is true drink. He who eats My flesh and drinks My blood abides in Me, and I in him [John 6:53-56, NASB].

Instead of weakening his approach under the pressure of rejection, he grew more explicit, as if to clarify where his listeners stood. Those who followed Jesus as they would any popular figure were dismayed and repulsed.

Many therefore of His disciples, when they heard this said, "This is a difficult statement, who can listen to it?" . . .

As a result of this many of His disciples withdrew, and were not walking with Him anymore [John 6:60, 66, NASB].

Vital communication assures not only acceptance, but rejection. It draws the line between unbelief and belief, between human opinion and divine truth. True communication ends not in words but in life. Jesus responded,

It is the Spirit who gives life; the flesh profits nothing; the words that I have spoken to you are spirit and are life [John 6:63, NASB].

Jesus began with the masses on the grassy slopes surrounding the sea of Galilee. He met their need for food and stimulated their interest in his message. In the fourth stage of communication, instead of facing the throng, he faced twelve men, one of whom would betray him. "Jesus said therefore to the twelve, 'You do not want to go away also, do you?' " (John 6:67, NASB). Jesus, the communicator, allowed his eternal word to run its course. He knew how to deal with rejection and he was prepared to nurture the minority who believed. Are we prepared to communicate the gospel as Jesus did? Can we compassionately meet men's needs, declare the gospel without manipulation or compromise, and build the Church with men and women who confess as Peter did:

Lord to whom shall we go? You have words of eternal life. And we have believed and have come to know that You are the Holy One of God [John 6:68, 69, NASB].

7
MATERIALISM:
THE ENDLESS CRAVE

The modern industrial society in which we live is vastly
different from the agriculturally oriented society of
first-century Palestine. In the Bible we read of fishermen
and farmers, stories of sheep and sparrows, sermons
delivered on grassy slopes and mountain tops, treasures
hidden in the field, harvests that were ripe for the picking,
and laborers in the vineyard. At first glance we may think
that the Bible does not speak to the economic concerns of
our day. The question this raises is an important one. Is
the gospel of Jesus Christ truly relevant in an affluent,
highly industrialized society? Answering this question
will decide not only our position on the matter, but it will
determine our action.

THE QUESTION OF RELEVANCY
Just because the standard of living changes does not
mean that the nature of man changes. We usually think of
the technological and industrial disparity between the
first century and twentieth century in terms of the great
stretch of time which separates them. As if to say that
2,000 years of social evolution transformed man himself
instead of just the structure of society. There are greater
economic differences *within* today's world than there are

between the economics of first-century Jerusalem and
twentieth-century New York City. The distance between
economic systems is measured not only in centuries but
also in hours. I can leave my home today and tomorrow be
trekking through tropical jungles inhabited by
"uncivilized" Indians whose only means of livelihood
consists of hunting, fishing, and a few hand-planted crops.
The relevance of the gospel is not measured by culture's
standard of living. Regardless of the time period or type
of economic development, man shows a common human
nature and spiritual need. Two Harvard professors, Alex
Inkels and David Smith, concluded from their research
into a variety of twentieth-century cultures that man
exhibits a common human nature, no matter what his
cultural background.

*Without denying the uniqueness of each culture, we wish
to affirm the common human nature of the people who
make up each of these diverse societies. These separate
cultures do not alter the basic principles which govern
the structuring of personality in all men. We believe
certain panhuman patterns of response persist in the
face of variability in culture content.* [1]

Karl Marx disagreed. He believed that man's nature was
determined by his relation to the means of production.

*The mode of production in material life determines the
general character of the social, political, and spiritual
processes of life. It is not the consciousness of men that
determines their existence, but, on the contrary, their
existence that determines their consciousness.* [2]

History has proven, however, that a change in the social
order does not change the nature of man. The man who
supposedly shares ownership of the means of production
with his fellow workers is no different than the employee
in a factory owned by a few wealthy individuals. A new
economic order does not create a new man. The very idea
that it does is only an illusion which hinders the
acceptance of the gospel. Josif Ton, a Baptist pastor in
Ploesti, Romania, expresses the expectation of the
Marxist-Leninist teachers:

*They were convinced that a radical and essential change
of man's character would happen automatically once
the economic, political, and social systems were altered.*

Ton continues,

*Today many years after the revolution has passed, it is
clear that socialist man's character has not changed. He
has remained as he was in the capitalist society; an egotist,
full of vice, and devoid of uprighteousness. It follows that
the creation of the new man still remains today a burden
to be realized, the fulfillment of which is forever
encountering obstacles.* [3]

The gospel is relevant to our industrialized society
because the nature of man has not changed. Furthermore,
Jesus has shown through his teaching that the gospel is
relevant to our economic era. He emphasized the
relationship between economics and a man's knowledge
of God.

Jesus did not say as Marx did that a man's nature is
transformed by a change in the economic order, but he did
say that what a man does or does not do with his money
demonstrates whether or not he has been transformed.
Zaccheus was a case in point (Luke 19:1-10). It would be
difficult to find someone whom the lower classes despised
more. Possibly the people of the Third World look at us in
much the same way that the poor people of Jericho looked
at Zaccheus. Certainly there are many complex reasons
for the low standard of living in underdeveloped countries,
ranging from political corruption and inadequate natural
resources to working habits and tropical heat. But one fact
which must be considered is the exploitation of the poor
nations by the wealthy nations. Zaccheus's corruption was
blatantly obvious to all. The mere recognition of him by
Jesus must have caused many to conclude that Jesus, like
most men, could be manipulated by money.
Notwithstanding, Jesus made a point of addressing this
needy man: "Zaccheus, come down immediately. I must
stay at your house today" (Luke 19:5, NIV). I wonder what
thoughts went racing through Zaccheus's head as he
climbed down out of the sycamore tree. Did it occur to him,

as it had to the people, that Jesus was paying attention to him because of his wealth and power? We have no idea from the biblical account, but we know that any such thought was quickly proven wrong. What Jesus impressed upon Zaccheus must be judged by Zaccheus's response.

Look, Lord! Here and now I give half of my possessions to the poor, and if I have cheated anybody out of anything, I will pay back four times the amount [Luke 19:8, NIV].

Did Zaccheus buy his salvation? What are we to make of Jesus' words to him?

Today salvation has come to this house, because this man, too, is a son of Abraham. For the Son of Man came to seek and to save what was lost [Luke 19:9, 10, NIV].

Zaccheus's lostness was not measured by the amount of wealth he possessed. It was measured by his relationship to God. Jesus came to save men like Zaccheus, to restore them to fellowship with God and to forgive their wrongdoing. Zaccheus's action was a response to salvation. Because he truly believed, he desired to demonstrate what Jesus meant to him. Without a transformation, there would have been no such demonstration.

Consider the rich young ruler who sadly turned away from Jesus because Jesus demanded that he sell all his possessions, give the money to the poor, and follow him. The request must have stunned the young man. How could Jesus ask such an outlandish thing? After all, had not God blessed him with this wealth? What sense was there to give it up? Interestingly enough, the man did *not* debate with Jesus. He did not argue that the command was senseless or unjustified. He turned his back on Jesus; not in disgust, but in sadness. Here was a man who knew the attractiveness of wealth.

There are two things that ought to impress us in these and other instances in which Jesus speaks of money. First, Jesus always relates the issue of money and possessions to himself. Our use of material wealth is meant to demonstrate Christ's Lordship. Second, Jesus makes us mindful of the eternal consequences of our use or misuse of earthly possessions. Jesus had a great deal to say about money and its influence on people. Economic change has not reduced the relevance of his teaching. If anything, Jesus' words are more appropriate today than ever before.

The reason is quite simple. If possessions and the desire for material security were barriers *then* to faith in Christ and true discipleship, how much more are they today! Jesus' words are not dismissed because they are irrelevant, but because they are too radical. They are *so* relevant that we prefer to make their meaning abstract. The Bible *does* speak to the economic concerns of our day. Its message knows no economic barrier. Man is in need of the good news, regardless of his standard of living. Jesus' teaching is not tied to an agrarian culture or a first-century economy. The deceptive idolatry of materialism is an even greater obstacle to man's salvation today than it was in the first century.

The Christian is called upon not only to agree that the gospel is indeed relevant to a modern industrial society, but he is also called to live on the basis of what Jesus taught. Spiritual and intellectual conviction must lead to practical application. Implementing biblical principles is not easy, but it is crucial for the effectiveness of the gospel. Our response to a materialistic life-style is indicative of our spiritual maturity. If the people we associate with know anything about Jesus and his teaching, they must wonder at our world-conforming life-style. There is a tendency among us to ignore many of the practical questions that arise out of our economic and industrial situation. Satan's influence is subtly exerted upon the Christian in exactly those areas which appear innocuous to our relationship with Christ. Is Christ concerned with our use of leisure time, with our attitude toward our employer, with the type of car and home we buy? Yes, I believe he is because such practical matters reflect the extent of Christ's Lordship over our lives.

Some time ago I was with a group of pastors discussing the needs of our churches. One man was especially

concerned to reach out to the new black community
moving into his church's neighborhood. The whites were
moving out rapidly and the market value of the property
was declining. This influx of blacks and the one or two
black families that had begun to attend the church
encouraged the zeal of the new pastor to begin a visitation
program. The pastor's attitude was commendable, but
one economic matter disturbed me. When the pastor took
responsibility of the church several months before, he
bought a house in a white suburb well outside the changing
community near the church. He said he did so because of
the depreciating value of the homes around the church and
his understanding that the schools were better farther
out. He was truly concerned to reach out to the
neighborhood, but he failed to do the most meaningful
and the most practical thing, namely, actually to live with
the people to whom he was burdened to minister.
Obviously from any other perspective than discipleship, the
pastor's choice to live outside the community was the
smart move, but the Christian response should have been
to locate near the church and the people he sought to
reach. Does this view seem judgmental and unrealistic to
you? It is not meant to be. The purpose is to illustrate the
practical consequences of following Christ, disregarding
personal, economic loss.

There is a crisis in the North American church today
because of our absorbing preoccupation with material
things. We have failed, and are failing, to relate the gospel
to our life-style. I am persuaded that the evangelical
church must confront the crisis of a materialistic life-style
with practical, church-oriented action.

THE CRISIS OF ALLEGIANCE

*No one can serve two masters. Either he will hate the
one and love the other, or he will be devoted to the one and
despise the other. You cannot serve both God and money*
[Matthew 6:24, NIV].

Single-minded obedience is for many the Christian
ideal rather than the normal course of discipleship.

However, Christ's words are unmistakably clear. We can
not serve God *and* our materialistic self-interests. There is
no excuse for making abstract what Jesus intended to be
clear and simple. He added these pointed words,

*For this reason I say to you, do not be anxious for your
life, as to what you shall eat, or what you shall drink; nor
for your body, as to what you shall put on. Is not life
more than food, and the body than clothing?* [Matthew
6:25, NASB].

Jesus speaks here of life's necessities: food and clothing.
Jesus is telling us not even to be concerned with the
basics of life, let alone the luxuries. Obviously, the call of
Christ is to a *new existence.* No one would dare transform
his priorities as Christ tells him he must unless he has
truly met Jesus Christ and has been transformed by him.
The crisis of allegiance affects both the poor and the rich. A
believer does not need to be wealthy to let material things
get in the way of his relationship to Christ. The issue is not
the ascetic life, but allegiance to Christ. The call of
Christ is not to inactivity or passivity, but to a life of faith.
Work can become a way of clinging to one's own destiny
by relegating spiritual security to a state of mind and
advancing economic stability as the practical goal of life.
When this occurs the avenue of faith becomes small and
narrow, one that can be easily bypassed in the fast flow of
our self-made plans.

The primary issue that confronted the rich young ruler
(Luke 18) was the Lordship of Christ. The practical issue was
between affluence and poverty. These two cannot be
divorced. That is not to say all possessions must be sold in
order to believe, but it does say that the whole of life
must be opened to faith in Christ. What was at stake in
Christ's challenge was a *transformation of values.* The
rich young ruler was called to follow an entirely new path:
away from self and toward Christ, from leading to
following, from leisure to cross bearing. The man was faced
with a crisis of allegiance. W. Herbert Scott of World
Vision International writes,

*Christians . . . need to re-examine the scriptural injunctions
on their world-responsibility. It seems we have become one*

with the world in our love for material things and for economic security. Even those in "full-time Christian service" jest about "suffering hardship for Jesus." Few of us really know experientially the reality and blessing of full commitment to God of all we are and have.[4]

THE CRISIS OF POSSESSIONS

If we were to interpret John 10:10 ("I have come that they may have life and have it to the full," NIV) from the perspective of the average North American believer, we would have to conclude that Jesus' original disciples missed out on quite a bit. Today's "abundance" includes Christ *and* possessions. Or does it? Are the things we own indications of blessing or a curse? Let's face the issue squarely! What right has the Christian to live as a materialist; to be possessed by his possessions (real or imaginary)? Can we continue to rationalize our high standard of living by saying, "If God didn't want me to have it, he would not have given me the money to get it"? Possessions do not free us, they enslave us. Dietrich Bonhoeffer expressed it well:

Be not anxious! Earthly possessions dazzle our eyes and delude us into thinking that they can provide security and freedom from anxiety. Yet all the time they are the very source of all anxiety. If our hearts are set on them, our reward is an anxiety whose burden is intolerable. Anxiety creates its own treasures and they in turn beget further care. When we seek for security in possessions we are trying to drive out care with care, and the net result is the precise opposite of our anticipations. The fetters which bind us to our possessions prove to be cares themselves.[5]

Physical provision is necessary for all men and promised by God to those who seek first his kingdom (Matthew 6:33). Jesus ate, drank, and was clothed in such a way as not to draw attention to his poverty. Luke reports that certain women financially supported Jesus and the twelve disciples (Luke 8:3). Material goods are not bad in themselves. The difficulty lies in drawing a line between *legitimate use* and *"unlawful accumulation."*[6] And it is easy to have such an inflated notion of unlawful accumulation that everything but a palace, yacht, and private jet are legitimate. The crisis of possessions challenges us to review our life-style and motives by the Word of God and the Church. In Christ's parable of the rich fool it is evident that the man's only reference was to himself. Our rationalizations of excessive and inappropriate spending stem from the same egocentric root,

And he began reasoning to himself, saying, "What shall I do, since I have no place to store my crops?" And he said, "This is what I will do: I will tear down my barns and build larger ones, and there I will store all my grain and my goods" [Luke 12: 17, 18, NASB].

No thought is given to anyone else but himself. What about the people who tilled the land and harvested the crops? Or the poor who needed food? The decision of the rich man was a private matter. He would have defended his right to do his own thing in the same modern spirit characteristic of western individualism.

I will say to my soul, "Soul, you have many goods laid up for many years to come; take your ease, eat, drink, and be merry" [Luke 12:19, NASB].

The Christian may not be as blunt as this man, but the same rationale hangs over him. Real accumulation or even just the desire to accumulate distorts our priorities. The words of Jesus are clear: ". . . where your treasure is, there will your heart be also" (Matthew 6:21, NASB). But the meaning is lost when we conveniently spiritualize the "treasure." We convince ourselves that the abundance of things we possess does not jeopardize our interior commitment to Christ. We would condemn with vigor the blending of Christian truth with pagan idolatry, but we see nothing wrong with joining the treasure of material wealth with the treasure of Christian commitment. As if to suggest that an "eat, drink, and be merry" philosophy of life mixes well with the cross of Jesus Christ. God's verdict on the rich fool distinguishes between the temporal and the eternal, between legitimate use and unlawful accumulation, between love and greed:

You fool! This very night your soul is required of you; and now who will own what you have prepared? So is the man who lays up treasure for himself, and is not rich toward God [Luke 12:21, NASB].

THE PRINCIPLE OF EQUALITY

It is a remarkable fact that it could be said of the early Church that "there was not a needy person among them" (Acts 4:34). As needs did arise more wealthy members sold their possessions and gave the money to the apostles to distribute. From day one the Church was conscious of its unique opportunity and responsibility to be a sharing community. The Church could never have legislated such radical giving. It arose spontaneously as a result of the work of the Holy Spirit and the mature conviction of the early believers. In Acts we are not offered a system to follow, but practical goals to be achieved.

The kind of sharing which was so natural among early believers is foreign to us. Our *privacy* discourages an openness on economic matters. What *we* make financially is our own business. Yet honesty is a must if the Church is to know and meet needs. In recent years pressure has increased for politicians to disclose their sources of income in order to ensure that policy decisions are made without conflict of interest. If people can demand openness among their government officials, why can't the Church demonstrate a similar openness? Do we conceal our abundance to placate our conscience and thus reduce the pressure to meet the needs of others? *Demanding* openness would only mean failure, but think of the success where brothers equal before the Lord could share their supply and their need. Instead of concealed wealth there would be shared wealth.

Not only privacy, but also pride serves to disrupt Christian sharing. There is the pride of the wealthy believer who gives in order to control or to be honored and the pride of the needy man who begrudges being on the receiving end. The "rags to riches" ideal of the industrious, hard-working North American robs us of practical involvement in one another's lives. The man who has made it may say to the man in need, "I've experienced the struggle you are going through. It's good experience. It will strengthen you, deepen you." While another man may say, "I've experienced the struggle you're going through. Let me help you out." Now I ask you, which man is a brother to the one in need? Is it any wonder that most of us continue to foster the ideal of the self-made man? Having experienced the "struggle" we are ready to sit back in comfort and watch the next generation make it on its own.

There are problems in sharing. Motives must be weighed, goals have to be analyzed, and merit should be considered. However, the difficulties should not leave us indifferent to meeting an individual's needs. Some time ago, a young man was ordained in a church I was attending. He grew up in a non-Christian home, accepted Christ, and felt called of God to go to seminary. He was a capable and diligent student, but he lacked enough money to pay his way through. There was no question of either his need or his qualifications, but our help as a church was minimal. We received a letter from the seminary explaining his financial need and requesting that we help by matching what the school had already given. I remember the deacon-board discussion on the matter. All sorts of problems were raised. If we helped him out, what about financial aid to other students from the church? Should we show favoritism to the seminary student and ignore the biology student? What if he ended up in some other kind of work? Rather than seeing an opportunity, we saw a problem. Certainly, determining need and treating situations individually and fairly takes skill and sensitivity, but it is to our own disadvantage if we fail to give at all.

Giving is a gracious work, a ministry of stewardship carried on by all believers. Paul put it this way to the Corinthians:

For this is not for the ease of others and for your affliction, but by way of equality—at this present time your abundance being a supply for their want, that their abundance also may become a supply for your want, that there may be equality [2 Corinthians 8:13, 14, NASB].

What a change this would bring if we took Paul's advice seriously. If today's Christian honestly believed that all he has comes from God and belongs to God there would be an end to our economic caste system. The missionary and the executive would see economics in the same light. Excuses would be answered with actions. Does inequality exist because the Lord wants to keep the missionary especially sensitive to his dependency upon him, but disregards how the Christian executive saves or spends his money? Is the Lord deficient in his provision for the missionary and overly gracious to the executive, or has he provided for the missionary through the income that he has given the executive?

The Church cannot afford to have one believer restricting his ministry because of little financial support while permitting another believer to spend thousands of dollars on an item purely for personal pleasure. Paul used the experience of the Israelites in the wilderness to illustrate the principle of equality. He quotes from Exodus 16:18: "He who gathered much had nothing over, and he who gathered little had no lack." The manna was God's provision for the Israelites. It was supplied equally to all. No one could say that they had *earned* their manna. They had all received it from the hand of God. In spite of God's warning, some of the Israelites hoarded the manna, gathering more than they needed for their daily needs. As a result the manna "bred worms and stank" (Exodus 16:20). Material things can easily be turned into waste if they are not distributed properly.

Someone has summed up the principle of equality in this way: "The question is not are you living beyond your financial means, but are you living beyond the financial means of the body of Christ?" Transforming our giving pattern and life-style according to the teaching of Jesus is no easy task. The crisis of allegiance and the crisis of possessions are not issues resolved once and for all. We wage a continual struggle to respond sacrificially in a culture given over to the idolatry of things. The authority of the gospel to speak to twentieth-century man is made clear by a fellowship of believers who demonstrate in love what it means to give and to receive.

The Apostle Paul used money way beyond its dollar value and we should do the same. His refusal to take money from some churches established the purity of his motives. His encouragement of the Gentile churches to give to the Jerusalem church gave practical meaning to Christian unity. Paul used money as a tool to serve God's purposes. The end product paid lasting dividends.

8

THE ANSWERS
WE DON'T GIVE

The paralytic and his four companions expected an
answer from Jesus. Finding it was impossible to push
through the throng which filled the small house where
Jesus was speaking, they dug up the roof and let down their
friend on a stretcher. His need could not have been more
obvious. Mark does not tell us what the crowd's reaction
was to this unusual demonstration, whether there was
hushed silence or critical murmuring; but one thing was
undoubtedly certain. All eyes were turned toward Jesus to
see his reaction.

Then Jesus did what must have confused some and
angered others. He looked into the expectant eyes of a man
whose health was hopeless and said, "My son, your sins
are forgiven." The religious leaders objected. Who was
Jesus of Nazareth when it came to forgiving a man's sin?
"Why does this man speak that way? He is blaspheming;
who can forgive sins but God alone?"

The man remained paralyzed, but not for long. Jesus,
pressing the proof of his authority to meet man's
physical and spiritual needs, immediately responded,

Why are you reasoning about these things in your hearts?
Which is easier, to say to the paralytic, "Your sins are
forgiven"; or to say, "Arise, and take up your [bed] and
walk"? [Mark 2:8, 9, NASB].

Jesus does not equate this man's need for forgiveness with his need to walk. However, he does use physical restoration to show his authority to bring about the salvation of the whole man. He placed both the physical and the spiritual need under his Lordship.

But in order that you may know that the Son of Man has authority on earth to forgive sins . . . I say to you, rise, take up your [bed] and go home [Mark 2:10, 11, NASB].

Jesus answered this man as only the Son of God could—with forgiveness and healing. His words have tremendous importance to us living in the twentieth century. If the world is to believe that the Son of Man has power to forgive sins, we must demonstrate a compassion for man's physical needs and the ability to meet those needs.

Our discipleship must take Jesus' example seriously. The world is at our door. Needy men and women are pressing us for a demonstration of God's love. Can we afford to become lost in the crowd and turn a deaf ear to the heart cry of those in need? The world has a right to question the authenticity of self-confessed evangelicals who respond to people in a worldly way. Are we any different than the priest and the Levite who passed by their Jewish brother who was beaten and bloody in the road (Luke 10:30)? Are we making excuses or are we compassionately self-sacrificing? The needs of individuals around us and the world at large are as obvious as the paralyzed man let down through the roof or the beaten man on the roadside. The media eye searches every corner of our global village, exposing us to overwhelming human needs. What is the Christian answer? Is it indifference or is it fear that but for the grace of God we would also be in poverty and famine? Can we help it if we are blessed with abundance while many others barely survive? Western individualism and a self-preserving isolation influences the mood of evangelicals far more than the Word of God. "Whatever will be will be" and the "survival of the fittest" are more appropriate slogans to match our actions than the principle of the cross: "My life for yours."

The answers we don't give cover a broad range of practical issues from eating habits to business practices, from the use of our wealth to the proper use of our citizenship. The domain of Christ's good news knows no boundaries. The Christ of the gospel is alienated from the world-conforming, world-ignoring church. Jesus warned us of "sand castle" evangelicalism.

Why do you call Me, "Lord, Lord," and do not do what I say? . . . the one who has heard, and has not acted accordingly, is like a man who built a house upon the ground without any foundation; and the river burst against it and immediately it collapsed, and the ruin of that house was great [Luke 6:46-49, NASB].

In the pages to follow, we will deal with the social implications of the gospel and what the wholistic gospel of Jesus Christ ought to mean to today's Christian.

THE CRISIS OF MINISTRY

The criticism that Jesus ignored culture is unjustified. Indeed, he was indifferent to the limitations imposed by political structures and social prejudice. But by ignoring such matters he was free to meet people's needs, both spiritual and physical. The Bible does not divide man into a religious being and a social being. Man is neither a body-less soul nor soul-less body. He is both body and soul. True evangelism meets the needs of the whole man. Preaching the gospel and making provision for man's physical needs are two distinguishable tasks, but neither can be separated from the other. Believers are not called upon to choose between a spiritual gospel and a social gospel. Such a dichotomy is foreign to both the teaching and example of Christ. In the mind of Jesus, a denial of man's physical needs either outrightly or passively, was inconsistent with man's identity as the image-bearer of God.

Do not work for the food which perishes, but for the food which endures to eternal life, which the Son of Man

*shall give to you, for on Him the Father, even God, has set
His seal* [John 6:27, NASB].

Do these words deny Jesus' social concern? Not at all. The
day before he had fed these same people. He had already
demonstrated his compassion for their physical needs. But
now, it was *necessary* to address an even more important
need.

The world can never balance man's spiritual and
physical needs. No matter how hard it tries its answers
fall short. Neither the mystic nor the political
social reformer are adequate to the task. If the spiritual
dimension is divorced from man's physical and
psychological needs the result is a Pharasaic piety. In Jesus'
day the sentiment of the religious elite was especially
bent in this direction. Instead of serving the people, the
Pharisees oppressed the people. Spirituality was equated
with religiosity. What mattered most was how a man
related to the Temple and the ceremonial law. True
spirituality was replaced by an institutional religion which
ignored man as man and served its own self-interests. On
the other hand, if the physical dimension is divorced from
man's need for forgiveness and a right relationship with
God, the result is a hollow social activism. It is empty
because there is no meaning or direction to the action.
Man has no more value than an animal and even less than
some endangered species. Ideologies and political parties
which ostensibly begin with only man's physical needs in
view quickly demonstrate an inherent disdain for man as
man.

Nominal Christianity, North America's public
religion, has been responsible for perpetuating this false
dichotomy. Many individuals are a happy blend of
religious piety and social activism, neither of which are
guided by the Word of God. Spiritually there is an
unwillingness to accept the truth the Bible proclaims,
making Christianity little more than a good tradition to
observe and a feeling of "worship" to experience. Culturally
there is an unwillingness to apply the teaching of the
Bible to morality, ethics, and life-style. Thus, the nominal

Christian is left with only the valueless vestiges of true religion.

It is not difficult to see why theologians reacted against this "know nothing, do nothing" kind of religion. Walter Rauschenbusch was one such theologian. He popularized what came to be know as the "social gospel." He emphasized the need for social justice and the rearrangement of the economic order. According to Rauschenbusch, Jesus advocated social reconstruction in place of spiritual redemption. The circumstances of history gradually caused Jesus' followers to become more preoccupied with spiritual concerns than with man's socio-political situation. Rauschenbusch reinterprets the gospel:

But as the eternal life came to the front in Christian hope, the kingdom of God receded to the background, and with it went much of the social potency of Christianity. The kingdom of God involved the social transformation of humanity. The hope of eternal life, it was held, was the desire to escape from this world and be done with it. The kingdom was a revolutionary idea; eternal life was an ascetic idea. [1]

To side with Rauschenbusch is to conclude that Jesus died a disappointed social reformer and that the apostles "missed the boat" in their emphasis upon sin and redemption. Today we can fault the impotency of the believer to meet the physical and spiritual needs of men, but we can not fault the gospel. The emphasis of the gospel has not evolved from the physical to the spiritual, or the practical to the ascetic, or the political to the religious. The gospel has never known such a dichotomy even though both liberal and conservative theologians have been guilty of distorting the truth.

A contemporary reaction paralleling the social gospel is the "Theology of Liberation." Its advocates are mostly theologians from the Third World who are calling for an end to economic oppression. There is a growing number of evangelical leaders who are also calling for economic and political change in the Third World, but their theology is different from the theology described in *Time* magazine's report:

The Theology of Liberation in fact combines Marxist economic analysis with the teachings of the Old Testament prophets and the commands of the Christian gospel to fashion a demanding spiritual ethic: that it is every Christian's duty to fight oppression, especially industrial capitalism, which is viewed by this theology as the central evil today.[2]

For some liberation theologians the duty to fight oppression extends to the violent overthrow of the capitalistic system. While cherishing Marx's analysis of man's fundamental needs, they label their plans for political restructuring with the language of the Christian religion. Liberation is economic liberation. In order to encourage political action, Bibles are printed with pictures of political activists and explanatory footnotes. For example, in a Cuban edition Fidel Castro insisted that a photo of a mass political rally complete with a portrait of Lenin be inserted. The photo caption reads, "The believer participates in political life and searches, under any regime, for the society which gives dignity to all."[3]

Both the Theology of Liberation and the social gospel have their roots in Christianity. Their proponents have seen the desperate social needs of men and have responded with religious humanism. The same reasons that account for their popularity also suggest their dangers:

1. It is easier to meet a calculated physical need than it is to meet a spiritual need. At the very least, physical needs can be reckoned in dollars and cents, and at the most, a violent political revolution will cost lives instead of dollars. The needs are visual and the solutions are economic and political. But man's need for God cannot be conceptualized in the same way. No amount of money or political change can be substituted for a man's personal decision to follow Christ. Thus, without diminishing the importance of man's physical needs and in fact emphasizing the believers' responsibility to meet such needs, the Bible clearly places the highest importance on a

man's relationship to God through Christ. If the calculated physical needs supplant man's basic spiritual need, the gospel has lost its *human* importance. No matter how vital the humanitarian spirit or how visible the material results, motivation will not be sustained.

2. Instead of defining sin as man's personal rebellion against God, sin is seen as an environmental phenomenon. In the first instance man is no longer confronted with the truth of God's gracious provision for salvation. In the second instance, he is no longer confronted with the truth about himself. Sin is rationalized and defined in terms of the victimized, underprivileged, and the oppressive wealthy. Revolutionizing political structures is advertised as the solution to man's needs. There is a failure to acknowledge that the human dilemma exists equally as well in poverty as it does in plenty. The problem of sin and depravity are easily sidestepped when man's physical needs become the sole concern.

3. The Christianization of culture displaces the goal of making disciples of Jesus Christ. (Christianization puts a Christian gloss over pagan man.) With a deficient understanding of the gospel and sin, the object of change becomes the mass of humanity. Social reconstruction replaces personal spiritual transformation. Cultural change becomes an end in itself.

President Coolidge is reported to have said, "The man who builds a factory, builds a temple; and the man who works there, worships there."[4] No matter what the brand of social alleviation, the industrial smokestacks will faithfully burn incense to the gods of the twentieth century. Possessions and power will always be the world's priority. No economic system or worldly philosophy of life can change that. Jesus Christ did not come to reorganize man, but to redeem man; to offer true forgiveness and life. The Lordship of Christ is twentieth-century man's only wholistically authentic, eternally important alternative.

Speaking at the National Prayer Breakfast in Washington, Senator Mark Hatfield described the conflict.

*Today our abundance, which has brought material
blessings to so many, threatens us spiritually as a peril.
Never have we known such wealth, but never have we
worshipped wealth more. Dazzled by material success, we
have developed a new religion: the worship of progress.
We have placed our faith in technology, and devoted
increasing billions to life-destroying arsenals. Whereas
people once looked toward God for salvation, our culture
now propels them toward the domination of nature and
fellow human beings in a ceaseless quest for material
accumulation. The search for the transcendent,
mystical, supernatural reality of life is being supplanted by
religious devotion to what is visible, tangible, and
synthetic. From such bondage Jesus Christ yearns to set us
free.*[5]

Clarifying the weakness of the social gospel does not remove
the evangelical's social responsibility. If anything, it
intensifies it. The title of this chapter, "The Answers We
Don't Give" is meant not for the liberation theologians,
but for the twentieth-century evangelical. Theological
positions can be twisted and distorted by the cultural
context. True theology demands that we be discerning,
judging movements on the basis of the whole Word of
God. But with that said, true theology demands more than
intellectual conviction. Our deficiency is measured not
by the correctness of our views, but by our failure to obey
the Word of God. The *truth* of Jesus Christ demands that
we preach *and* live the Word of God. Personal conviction
and commitment are foundational to new life in Christ.
The Word must be heard and confession made. But at the
same time the *love* of Christ dictates that we care for a
man's physical needs. The fruits of Christ's Lordship will
result in a clarification of sin, an expanded vision and a
changed life-style.

A CLARIFICATION OF SIN

Ask any evangelical what sin is and the answer he will give
will be that sin is rebellion against God. He will likely

quote from the prophet Jeremiah, "the heart is more deceitful than all else and is desperately sick" (Jeremiah 17:9, NASB), or from the prophet Isaiah, "All of us like sheep have gone astray, each of us has turned to his own way. . ." (Isaiah 53:6, NASB). The Bible presents God's verdict on man's depravity clearly. Just as clear is God's provision for man's salvation. Both sin and salvation are matters that involve the individual. Any attempt to abstract sin's reality or to politicize salvation runs against the truth of God's Word. However, most evangelicals are too narrow in their perspective of sin. While the personal-individualistic dimension of sin is emphasized, the broader cultural dimension of sin is ignored. Do we see sin as God sees sin? Are we willing to expose man's personal spiritual dilemma *and* the cultural impact of man's fall? In other words, does our acceptance of Jesus Christ as Lord involve more than a personal notion of forgiveness of sin?

Jeremiah's understanding of man's deceitfulness was wholistic. It incorporated man's personal interior rebellion as well as the external actions that flowed from man's depravity. Jeremiah began with man's heart and ended with man's culture. Sin meant immorality *and* materialism, idolatry *and* the neglect of widows and orphans, lying *and* social injustice. The sins of the individual and the sins of the society were attacked by Jeremiah without equivocation.

The prophet Amos declared:

For three transgressions of Israel, and for four, I will not revoke the punishment; because they sell the righteous for silver, and the needy for a pair of shoes—they trample the head of the poor into the dust of the earth, and turn aside the ways of the afflicted; a man and his father go into the same maiden so that my holy name is profaned [Amos 2:6, 7, RSV].

God does not excuse institutional evil any more than he excuses sexual immorality. What may appear socially acceptable and sanctioned by law may be nothing more than sin from God's perspective. It is much easier to isolate a few sinful deeds than to allow God's Word to expose the broad boundaries of sin. Our understanding of righteousness and evil must be determined by the Word of God. History has effectively demonstrated the influence tradition has had on shaping our idea of sin. Unless we hear the voice of God, modern man's enlightened rationalizations and legal maneuvering will determine for us what sin is. It must be acknowledged, however, that many Christians are so immersed in society's system that reading the Bible has little convicting impact.

One scene from the TV movie "Roots" illustrates this. With the sound of the foreman's whip cracking across the back of Toby, a young black slave, an old black slave begs to see the master. Grudgingly he is ushered into the study where the master is reading his Bible. The old slave pleads with the master, but to no avail; the beating of Toby goes on and the master goes back to reading his Bible. Society's impulse can be so strong that the Bible is sometimes used by well-meaning Christians to defend the prevailing injustices. Some have dismissed a great deal of the Old Testament teaching on injustice and materialism on grounds that it was directed at Israel. It is true that the Jubilee principle (Lev. 25:10-24) and the Sabbatical year (Lev. 25:2-7) were designed specifically for Israel as the people of God. In any government other than a theocracy such measures would be practically impossible. However, they do reveal to everyone the changeless mind of God. God alone is the absolute owner of property. Economic justice among all men is demanded. The dignity of man must not be sacrificed for materialistic gain. These principles coincide with the biblical right to private property and the blessing of God's creation (1 Tim. 4:1-4).

Jesus, who was neither an ascetic nor a materialist, calls us to follow him. If the Word of God is neglected or rationalized, we will define sin according to the habits of our subculture. Isaiah, Amos, and Jeremiah were men of God whose messages are one with the entire flow of biblical revelation in both the Old and New Testaments. But Israel was no more open to the biblical answers these

prophets offered than is today's technological culture
open to the answers evangelicals should offer. Are we willing
to let the Word of God permeate our thinking so that we
might permeate society? Is the Word of God a burning fire
shut up in our bones, impossible to be contained
(Jeremiah 20:9)?

Jesus told his disciples that the Holy Spirit would
"convict the world concerning sin, and righteousness, and
judgment" (John 16:8, NASB). The Holy Spirit was not
given to us as some feeling to be experienced, but as God
himself working through us in power and wisdom. The
Spirit trains us in the way of righteousness both in our
worship and our political decisions, in our business
practices as well as in the compassionate use of God's
blessings. We are dependent on the Word and Spirit of God
to discern what is truly sin and what is truly good in both
global issues, ranging from trade to nuclear armament,
and personal issues, such as our choice of entertainment and
eating habits. We must have God's view of sin if we are to
live as Christ's disciples.

AN EXPANDED VISION

Exposing injustices in the world and working in government
and business on the basis of biblical principles is surely
inconsistent if we are not practicing in the Church what
we demand in public. Many who read this will have
trouble identifying three poor families in their church. Not
because they have shared their abundance in order to
meet people's needs, but because of the high standard of
living and the suburban distribution of white evangelical
churches. Concerned with buildings, programs and staff, our
churches have all but forgotten the *majority* of our
brothers and sisters in Christ. Apparently distance makes
little difference, for we are as isolated from our inner-city
brothers as we are from our Third World brothers. We love
the practice of isolationism and the theory of the
worldwide Church. Our outlook on overseas giving is a
missionary's salary and money for buildings. But where
is our compassion? Where is our vision? We are not a

corporation extending loans to foreign subsidaries; we are a family offering love to Christ himself.

Jesus underscored the mark of a born-again believer when he told a parable illustrating the last judgment (Matt. 25:31-46). The "sheep" on his right hand and the "goats" on his left were distinguished by their practice. To the "sheep" the King declared,

Come, you who are blessed of My Father, inherit the kingdom prepared for you from the foundation of the world. For I was hungry, and you gave Me something to eat; I was thirsty, and you gave Me drink; I was a stranger, and you invited Me in; naked, and you clothed Me; I was sick, and you visited Me; I was in prison, and you came to Me [Matthew 25:34-36, NASB].

The righteous respond in surpise, "When did we see You [in need]?" And the King answers,

Truly, I say to you to the extent that you did it to one of these brothers of Mine, even the least of them, you did it to Me [Matthew 25:40, NASB].

The parable does not pretend to present the full doctrine of salvation. Nothing here distracts from the importance of belief in Christ. The emphasis is upon the visible manifestation of belief. Jesus Christ's identification with us in our need did not stop when he was lowered from the cross. He stands in the place of our needy brother ready to receive our offering of worship. Everything we give to our brother first of all passes through the King.

Whose recognition do we seek, Christ's or the world's? Robert Schuller, pastor of Garden Grove Community Church in California says openly what many Christians believe quietly:

We are trying to make a big, beautiful impression upon the affluent non-religious American who is riding by on this busy freeway. It's obvious that we are not trying to impress the Christians. . . . Nor are we trying to impress the social workers in the County Welfare Department. They would tell us that we ought to be content to remain in the Orange Drive-In Theatre and give the money to feed

*the poor. But suppose we had given this money to feed
the poor? What would we have today? We would still have
hungry, poor people and God would not have this
tremendous base of operations which He is using to
inspire people to become more successful, more
generous, more genuinely unselfish in their giving of
themselves.* [6]

Does the affluent suburbanite need a show of wealth in
order to be attracted to Christ? The answer is obvious.
The big, beautiful impression looks ugly from every
perspective except the world's. The rich Christian builds
his monuments while the poor Christian suffers.
Professional preachers in their posh galleries profane the
gospel as surely as the slave master studying his Bible with
the sound of a cracking whip in the background.

An enlarged vision means a greater sensitivity to the
whole Church. Without a compassionate response to
fellow Christians, our worship of God will suffer a
debilitating setback. The Christians at Corinth thought
they were celebrating the Lord's Supper. Paul disagreed.
Paul tells us that some believers were coming to the
Lord's table hungry and others were coming well fed. The
same class divisions which existed in society had crept
into the body of Christ. Paul did not take the situation
lightly. "Therefore whoever eats the bread or drinks the
cup of the Lord in an unworthy manner, shall be guilty of
the body and the blood of the Lord" (1 Corinthians 11:27,
NASB).

A local fellowship of believers cannot be vital in their
worship if they fail to recognize in love any member of the
body of Christ. Ronald Sider explains what this
recognition means.

*To discern the Lord's body is to understand and live the
truth that fellowship with Christ is inseparable from
membership in his body where our oneness in Christ far
transcends differences of race or class. Discernment of
that one body of believers leads to unlimited
availability to and responsibility for the other sisters and
brothers. Discernment of that one body prompts us to*

*weep with those who weep and rejoice with those
who rejoice. Discernment of that one body is totally
incompatible with feasting while other members of the
body go hungry. Those who live a practical denial of their
unity and fellowship in Christ, Paul insists, drink
judgment on themselves when they go to the Lord's
table. In fact they do not really partake of the Lord's Supper
at all.* [7]

In the parable of the talents, the faithless servant was
condemned for doing *nothing* (Matthew 25:14-30). He
did absolutely nothing except wait for his master to return.
His caution, mixed with laziness, rendered him useless.
The master could not afford even one talent to remain idle.
Do we have a vision of what God can do with the
material things he has given to us? Do we see our brothers
and sisters in Christ who suffer because of our failure to
act? The vision of a needy world is not an option for the
twentieth-century believer. The time is *now* for whole
churches to reassess their priorities and to implement
voluntary programs of living and giving which are
sacrificial instead of superficial. The proverb must be
heeded, "Where there is no vision the people perish"
(Proverbs 29:18).

A CHANGED LIFE-STYLE

*Truly I say to you, there is no one who has left house or
brothers or sisters or mother or father or children or
farms, for My sake and for the gospel's sake, but that he
shall receive a hundred times as much now in the present
age, houses and brothers and sisters and mothers and
children and farms, along with persecutions; and in the
world to come, eternal life* [Mark 10:29, 30, NASB].

Jesus spoke these words right after Peter had given the
clearest possible formula for changing one's life-style.
"Behold, we have left everything and followed You"
(Matthew 10:28, NASB). What did Jesus mean when he said
the believer shall receive a hundred times as much now in
the present age? If Jesus had said that we would receive a

hundred times as much in heaven, there would be no confusion. But he does not say heaven; he says "the present age." How can a rejection of loyalties and possessions be replaced by new relationships and new possessions? The answer is the *Church*! It is within the Church that we have been given a new family. The self-centered, every-man-for-himself existence yields to the interdependence of the fellowship of believers. The blessing of genuine community is neither just theory nor utopia. Neither lectures on community nor withdrawal from the world create the kind of blessing Jesus promised. No new theories or seminars are needed. The answer stares us in the face. If we follow Peter's example we will receive the promised hundred-fold.

Not long ago I talked with a Chinese graduate student about Christ. In the course of our conversation I asked him what would it mean in his life if he were to follow Christ. His answer surprised me. He said, "I would become weak because God would take care of everything." "Do you mean you would become lazy?" I asked. He replied, "Yes!" To him the Christian life meant an inner escape from the realities of life. I explained to Tony that Jesus calls us to redirect our whole lives according to his purposes. Reality is not escaped; it is confronted by a total life commitment to Christ in obedience to his revealed Word, the Bible.

Forsaking everything to follow Christ means Christ-like compassion for all those in hunger, especially members of our family in Christ. If we do not change our life-style, Christ's promise of blessing to Third World Christians is mockery. What can we expect the world to conclude about Christ if no compassionate, sacrificial answer to man's physical and spiritual needs is forthcoming from those who pledge loyalty to his name throughout North America? It is impossible to conclude that faith in Christ is an emotional crutch when Christians demonstrate costly Christ-like love.

Forsaking everything to follow Christ means Christ-like service. What should the world conclude when evangelical leaders carry over into the Church, the Christian college, the mission organizations, the Christian book publishers, or the Christian music companies the same ranking and salary incentives as a secular institution? Is it so unreasonable to think that Christ intended Bible College trustees to live on the same income as Bible College teachers? Christ did not promise more money for those who lead. He called for greater sacrifice. Leadership ability is measured by a man's closeness to the mind of Christ, not his profession or income. The life-style we wish to emulate does not belong to those *of* the world but to men and women *in* Christ.

Forsaking everything to follow Christ results in Christ-like motivation. Jesus was motivated by the will of the Father. It was not an admission of weakness, but the reason for his strength when he said, "The Son can do nothing of Himself, unless it is something He sees the Father doing; for whatever the Father does, these things the Son also does in like manner" (John 5:19, NASB). Do we dare reject the motivation Jesus desires to give us and in its place substitute the motivation of a new house or a higher position?

In a tongue-in-check editorial entitled "It's Our Duty to Live Beyond Our Means," *Toronto Star* reporter, Gary Lautens, writes,

What better incentive is there for a person to get ahead in the world than crushing debt?

If I hadn't been up to my hips in red ink, would I have stayed at the 9 to 5, would I have taken on extra jobs . . . would I have kept out of trouble, more or less, and been a good boy? Not very likely.

If I hadn't had this overwhelming desire to live over my head, to eat filet, when the pay stub was shouting "wienies!" in my ear, undoubtedly I'd still be sleeping in 'til noon, and so would you.

How else do you make progress if you don't bite off more than you can chew, and then scramble to catch up?[8]

The charge of escapism is seldom heard when a man truly forsakes the world for Christ. A more likely reaction was anticipated by Jesus. "He shall receive a hundred times as much now in the present age. . .*along with persecutions.*" What the world cannot tolerate is the world's greatest blessing. Christ has called the Church to answer the world in confidence and love with an uncompromising biblical view of sin, a compassionate vision of man's needs, and the means to meet those needs by a Christ-centered life-style. May we make Christ's answer plain to a needy world.

9
WILL THE
FAMILY SURVIVE?

The preceding chapters give us some idea of the pressures facing the modern family. Society's basic building block does not exist in a vacuum. There is no germ-free environment in which the family can grow. The influences of the media, materialism, and modular relationships take their toll on culture's front-line community. The family is much more than a biological or cultural social structure. It is a living community ordained by God for the purpose of giving to children and adults the experience of sacrificial love, wholistic training, and daily worship.

For many, the family is not a haven. It is a nightmare. The manipulation and meaninglessness of modern life do not vanish when parent and child are safely ensconced within the four walls of their suburban home. The pressures are not removed; they are intensified.

I believe that many who have rejected the family began by placing their highest expectations in the family. A happy marriage, two nice children, and a secure job was life's reasonable hope. But the expectation failed; not because people did not desire lasting human relationships, but because the basis for love and trust was shattered. The pressures of a materialistic and self-gratifying culture are too much for a "love" without commitment and for people without God. By rejecting God's truth on sex,

marriage, and child development, man is finding the
secure family an illusive dream. The family cannot survive
in any Christian sense among those who are convinced
that the family's origin and function are derived simply
from cultural convention and biological convenience.
The future does not look bright for this, society's
cornerstone. Philippe Ariès, an internationally known
historian of family life, projects the following hypothesis for
tomorrow's family:

*The undissolvable, monogamous community will persist,
but only during the woman's voluntary period of
fecundity and the education of the children. Let us say,
about 15 years. Before and after this period there will be
no stable community, no family. Each person will live
freely on his own.* [1]

The disintegration of the family has meant an increase in
divorce, premarital conceptions, illegitimate births,
abortions, and homosexuality. There is a growing number
of children with almost no parental care. Already more
than one-sixth of America's children are living in
single-parent families. The parent, usually a woman,
almost always works full time. In some of our cities, the
number of illegitimate births is greater than legitimate
births. Advocates of the new permissiveness argue that man
needs freedom. Conventional sex mores and family bonds
have to be changed if an individual is to cope with a highly
industrialized culture and the changing patterns of
human thought. They welcome the "opening up" of the
family. Men and women are free to do what they wish
without the restraint of an enduring commitment. But
such supporters are oblivious to the ruined lives, the
emotionally and physically spent people, the parentless
children, and the destitute elderly.

Philippe Ariès views our rejection of traditional family
ties as a defense against the increasingly confining world
system.

*. . . the revolt against the family is only an aspect of the
Western revolt against the technical society. It is the revolt*

of a prisoner who has lived in a confined world that is becoming narrower.[2]

In part, Ariès is correct. He claims that the automobile and TV have accentuated a "hideaway tendency." The nuclear family has become a "ghetto," insulating people from the realities of an industrial civilization. We no longer interact except within the "prison of love," the family. I am sure there are many unmarried Christians who would look at the families in their church and agree with Ariès. Where is the love and outreach which ought to characterize the Christian home? Why are families so wrapped up in their own little world that they have no time for anyone else? Evangelicals may be successful in upholding the sanctity of marriage, but they fail in demonstrating Christian love. Yet both are vitally important. We may righteously resist moral relativism while we subtly submit to a "closed" family. In the end our moral stand will be placed in jeopardy by a second or third generation intent on breaking out of the "prison." We wonder why Christian kids lack purpose and conviction. After all, they have grown up in nice homes, attended Sunday School and Christian youth groups, and have had an "open door" to college. Ariès puts his finger on one of the reasons. Life is very confining. It has been and continues to be *self-directed.* The family has existed in and for itself.

I do differ, however, with Ariès in one important respect. The revolt against the family is *not* a revolt against the technological society. The disintegration of the family is in fact a continuation of the system. The autonomy of the selfish family has been replaced by the autonomy of the lone individual. Instead of a ghetto of four or five, we have a ghetto of one unwed mother, or one elderly man, or one orphan. The tragedy of today's family did not take place overnight. The revolt against the family has been nurtured through so many successive stages that its true purpose and function are impossible for many to detect. We have somehow convinced ourselves that the sorry state of the family can be blamed on society's indifference, or poor education, or government policy. A whole host of "causes" excuses our dilemma; from unemployment and welfare to the lack of sex education, inadequate day-care centers and our high standard of living. The revolt against the family is essentially a revolt against the authority of God's Word. It is a revolt against knowable standards and true relationships.

THE REVOLT AGAINST KNOWABLE STANDARDS

The Old Testament uses three terms to describe sexual relationships: "to know," "to lie with," and "to go into." Apart from a few exceptions, these three phrases indicate respectively God's favor on the relationship, God's disfavor on the relationship, and the physical need to become pregnant.

"To know" expresses the *wholeness* God intended for the marriage relationship. A husband and wife formed a complete and permanent unity. By tossing God's standard aside, as if it were some cultural anachronism, modern man has cheapened marriage and himself. Sex has become a shallow, counterfeit experience. What was meant to be the "summit experience" of marriage, a celebration of past, present, and future total commitment, has become the flaunted banner of alienation and instant pleasure. William Willimon writes,

The so-called revolution against marriage is no revolution at all. It is merely one more example of our modern Western craving for instant gratification. We want everything right away, without risk or investment—from instant oatmeal to instant sex. We are a society of instant hedonists. The pursuit of pleasure, companionship, and sexual joys for their own sake is in fact an unconscious collaboration with "the system" at its worst rather than a rejection of it. [3]

Our capacity for commitment to God and one another has been eroded. Modern man's preoccupation with the present has had two ill effects on marriage and the family. First, today's men and women are convinced that principles based on God's Word cannot possibly hold true

in the twentieth century. The biblical concept of sin
belongs to another era. Guilt is reducible to silly hang-ups
and tradition-bound feelings. Having eliminated God's
moral standards, man has subjected his mind and
conscience to the instinctive rule of his physical
appetite. If sexual morality and marital fidelity are
preserved, it is for utilitarian reasons. The more
contemporary man subverts the will of God for the "good
of society," the worse society becomes.

Second, in the fast-flow world of technology and
materialism we have little patience for repetition and
permanence. According to anthropologist Margaret Mead,
no other society fears repetition and permanence the way
our society does. Other cultures consider what is permanent
to be trustworthy. But our society sees even the longevity
of life a problem.

*The safety valve of death has disappeared. The very
concept of divorce has changed. It was once a means to
resolve an unusual and irreparable situation. Today
divorce has become security for couples who cannot
tolerate each other for so many years. . . . Now that
yesterday's utopia is almost possible, we discover that one
hundred years together would be hell.*[4]

The paradox is forever staring us in the face. The more
we learn and adapt to God's physical laws, the less we
respect and tolerate God's laws for people. A scientist would
not think of dismissing a proven chemical or physical law
just because he did not like it. But we dismiss God's
standard for human relationships merely because it does
not suit us. The scientist does not create the laws of science,
but he does abide by them. Consider the folly of a group of
scientists on the brink of discovery deciding to junk their
experimental procedure. Instead of the laboratory, they
opt for the conference room. Because they cherish their
theory more than they seek reality, they decide to cut off
the experiment.

The modern revolt against the family is a rejection of
reality. In order for human relationships to be happy and
fulfilling, they must be guided by God's laws—a fact

modern man is unwilling to acknowledge. This does not
mean God's standards are cold and impersonal. They are
similar to physical properties in one important respect. The
same God who ordered creation made man. Matter has no
choice. All physical properties are obeyed automatically.
Man does have a choice. He can do his own thing in his
own way or he can choose to realize the value and dignity of
life through obedience to God's Word. Today's
disintegration of the family is a consequence of man's
disobedience. The biblical view of man resists cheap love
and empty relationships. People are not a commodity to be
bought and sold. Marriage is not merely a human contract
like some business deal. It is a "divine yoke," and the way
in which God lays "this yoke upon a married couple is
not so much by creating some kind of mystical union as by
declaring His will in His Word."[5]

The human values expressed in God's Word have been
replaced by man's inhuman values of "disposability,
expendability, and instant gratification."[6] The most serious
fact, however, is that modern man has grown accustomed
to his dilemma. He has accepted society's "new" values
and their consequences. There is no repentance or
sorrow. We handle the statistics of unwed mothers, divorce,
and abortion as casually as yesterday's football scores.
With dulled consciences we dispassionately speak of our
moral decline.

*As conventional marriage proves itself less and less capable
of delivering on its promise of life-long love . . . we can
anticipate open public acceptance of temporary marriages.
Instead of wedding "until death us do part," couples will
enter into matrimony knowing from the first that the
relationship is likely to be short lived. . . . While they may
yearn for a permanent relationship, something inside
whispers to them that it is an increasingly improbable
luxury.*[7]

The revolt against knowable standards is further
evidenced in the growing popularity of homosexuality. It is
argued that homosexuals are nice, respectable people.

Like other people, they should be allowed to do their own
thing. Who is to say what sexual activity is legitimate or
illegitimate? If a man is attracted to another man instead of
a woman, it is not going to affect anyone else. One kind
of sexual activity is just as right as another. With these
arguments, homosexuality is becoming more visible and
acceptable than ever before. At the heart of this new
acceptance is the modern autonomous man. God-given
standards of morality and behavior are gone.

The Bible is very clear in considering both sexual
immorality and homosexuality as sin. Paul's words against
homosexuality cannot be dismissed as ambiguous and
culturally conditioned.

*For this reason God gave them over to degrading
passions; for their women exchanged the natural function
for that which is unnatural, and in the same way also
the men abandoned the natural function of the woman and
burned in their desire towards one another, men with
men committing indecent acts and receiving in their own
persons the due penalty of their error* [Romans 1:26, 27,
NASB].

The New Testament deals with sexual sins in such a way
as to demonstrate the pervasiveness of the problem in the
first century. Neither popularity nor public approval
dissuaded Paul from judging homosexuality as a serious and
demeaning aberration of the divinely created sexual
structure. On the other hand, the Apostle Paul does not
single out homosexuals as a special category of sinners.

*Or do you not know that the unrighteous shall not inherit
the kingdom of God? Do not be deceived; neither
fornicators, nor idolaters, nor adulterers, nor effeminate,
nor homosexuals, nor thieves, nor the covetous, nor
drunkards, nor revilers, nor swindlers, shall inherit the
kingdom of God* [1 Corinthians 6:9, 10, NASB].

Both the homosexual *and* the thief required repentance
and forgiveness. Both the repentant homosexual and the
repentant adulterer were accepted into the church on the

basis of Jesus Christ's redemptive sacrifice. Apparently some of the members of the Corinthian church had been homosexuals; Paul finishes his thought in verse eleven:

And such were some of you; but you were washed, but you were sanctified, but you were justified in the name of the Lord Jesus Christ, and in the Spirit of our God [1Corinthians 6:11, NASB].

Christ confronts the homosexual with an acceptance which cannot be found in the world. Homosexuality is condemned, but the homosexual can be restored through Christ's love to a right relationship with God and his fellow man. The same can be applied to the immoral heterosexual.

Homosexual behavior is learned. There is no evidence that it has any genetic or hormonal cause. It usually can be traced to an unnatural child development where the mother allies with the son against the father, or the boy is made to feel unwanted or inferior by his mother or girls in his peer group.[8] Children are increasingly being brought up under abnormal conditions and becoming psychologically addicted to twisted sexual roles. Homosexuality is both a symptom and a cause of today's threatened family.

Finally, the revolt against knowable standards is evident in our failing reverence for life. The United Nation's declaration of human rights includes this important statement,

The child, by reason of its physical and mental immaturity, needs special safeguards and care, including appropriate legal protection before as well as after birth.[9]

That statement was issued in 1959. Today we are legislating against the child. The widespread acceptance of abortion is indicative of our moral decline. Our modern values of disposability, expendability, and instant gratification find their clearest and most serious expression in the very same institutions dedicated to the preservation of human life. Man's inhumanity to man has resulted in a culturally accepted, professionally enacted curtailment of life. In the

past, society has approved abortions only when the
mother's physical life was in jeopardy or when pregnancy
was the result of rape. Today, abortion is accepted by
many as a legitimate method of birth control. It is thought
to be merely another form of contraception. Women are
said to be the "victims" of pregnancy and threatened with
the responsibility of "unwanted children."

It appears that the mother's "right to privacy" was the
most important consideration in the 1973 U.S. Supreme
Court decision favoring abortion. The Court said, in effect,
that if a child is unwanted for any reason whatever, its life
may be aborted. With that decision, morality became a
matter of convenience. The baby was stripped of his
rights. No law protected him from D and C (dilation and
curettage), salt poisoning, or hysterotomy. Along with
society and his mother, he became a victim of modern
enlightenment. Is the life of an unborn baby any less real,
any less precious than the life of an adult patient lying on
the operating table? The modern mentality dictates that
the adult life is worth saving, at least today, but the baby's
life is not. Modern man no longer values the sacredness
of life. The validity of human existence is determined by a
changing code of ethics.

We no longer accept the social implications of
conception. The father has no rights. The child has no
rights. Even the rights of the mother are violated. Our
culture has placed such a high premium on man's
autonomous self-interests and the materialistic benefits of
the "good life" that the natural joys of raising a family
are subject to an unnecessary and often painful process of
decision making. In the twentieth century, motherhood
begins with the question, "Should I keep this baby?"

THE REVOLT AGAINST TRUE RELATIONSHIPS

This generation has succeeded in bringing the class
struggle into the home: husband versus wife, child versus
parent. The break-up of human relationships has resulted in
a deep and abiding sense of alienation. We are witnessing
a bloodless revolution. There is no guillotine lopping off

heads or terrorists running through the streets. But the upheaval is just as historically and socially real as any political war. I am not talking here about a woman's right to work, or the length of a teenager's hair. "Equal pay for equal work" and a young person's individuality are not small issues. But these concerns are not at the heart of the woman's liberation movement or the generation gap. The roots of our one-sided cultural emphasis on freedom, rights, equality, and independence can be traced to a fundamental dissatisfaction with ourselves and life in general. Our outward appearance of liberation could not be more deceiving. By contrast, the biblical emphasis on love, responsibility, and service cuts to the core the prevailing philosophy of life. "Your life for mine" is transformed by the principle of the Cross: "My life for yours."

Modern man is antagonized by the divinely inspired words of the Apostle Paul.

Wives, be subject to your own husbands, as to the Lord. . . . Husbands, love your wives, just as Christ also loved the Church and gave Himself up for her. . . .
Children obey your parents in the Lord, for this is right. . . . Fathers, do not provoke your children to anger; but bring them up in the discipline and instruction of the Lord [Ephesians 5:22, 25; 6:1, NASB].

The family is able to function properly only as its members operate according to God's appointed structure. Sexual differentiation is not a cultural convention. Paul's position is not a holdover from his rabbinic Judaism. It is based on God's created order. Before the Fall, God ordained a specific hierarchical family structure. Eve was created by God to be a helpmeet for Adam. Their equality before the Lord and their cohumanity were established at the same time as their differing roles.

Then the Lord said, "It is not good for the man to be alone; I will make him a helper suitable for him." . . . And the man said, "This is now bone of my bones, and flesh of my flesh; she shall be called Woman, because she was taken out of Man." For this cause a man shall leave his

father and his mother, and shall cleave to his wife; and
they shall become one flesh [Genesis 2:18, 23, 24,
NASB].

God's standards for sexual morality were established in
the created order. This means, as we have said, that
heterosexual attraction, the sanctity of sex in marriage,
and the permanence of the marriage bond are not culturally
conditioned mores, but enduring necessary truths. It
must also be said that God's structure for family
relationships—husband and wife, parent and child—are
based on the created order.

Adam is the "head" of Eve not because she is in any
way intellectually or physically inferior. She is not. Adam's
headship is determined, not earned. He is appointed and
Eve is appointed to a workable marriage relationship. Man is
the accountable head and woman is his helpmeet. After
the Fall, this existing relationship, along with the entire
created order, was subject to sin. The perfect balance of
authority and submission became subject to exploitation. To
advocate scrapping the differentiation between husband
and wife is as contrary to mankind's well-being as doing
away with work and child bearing. All three were
ordained by God before the Fall and all three were subject to
corruption because of the Fall. George W. Knight III offers
this important comment:

I agree that we should seek to relieve the effects of the
fall and sin in all three of those areas. But we do so not by
removing the realities altogether—childbirth, work, and
the role relationship of men and women—but by
alleviating that which corrupts the realities. For the
apostles and the New Testament, that means urging
husbands to love, honor, and not be bitter to their wives,
it does not mean urging them to cease being the head of
the household. The removal of an oppressive rule of a
husband over a wife is not the removal of headship and the
role relationship but the replacement of the effects of sin
in the role relationship by love. [10]

In radical terms, Paul proclaims the basis and extent of
redemptive unity in Galatians 3:28, "There is neither Jew

nor Greek, there is neither slave nor free man, there is neither male nor female; for you are all one in Christ Jesus." Does this statement disqualify the role relationship of men and women? Paul refers here to three commonly accepted cultural divisions: race, social position, and sex. The first two divisions between Jew and Gentile, slave and free man did not exist before the Fall. Animosity between races and social classes was a result of man's pride. However, the division between men and women can be seen in two ways. Role differentiation, as we have said, is supported by the created order, but sexual exploitation and the absence of mutual respect and love generated a second division. Paul's point is that "in Christ" the divisions generated through sin no longer divide the body of believers. Both men and women are restored to their true position as the image bearers of God. Elisabeth Elliot made this summary in an address given at Wheaton College.

What I have been saying is that in the secular world women are nearly interchangeable with men simply because neither men nor women are treated as whole persons. But the important distinction that Christians make is that women are assigned a special place in Church and home as opposed to in the secular world. In these two domains we return to reality. Women are treated as women, men as men, both sexes as whole persons, divinely created and divinely gifted, all of us complementary members of a single body, a mystical body when we are talking about the Church. [11]

The revolt against true relationships has affected not only the husband and wife, but also the parents and children. The class struggle between the young and old is not entirely the fault of a rebellious younger generation. Adults, not children, are responsibile for today's social structure. If the adult world is isolated from the children's world, it is not the fault of the children. Philippe Ariès writes,

In modern times, the child is separated from adult society and put apart in a space intended and specialized for

him: the school. . . . The contemporary family was born
when society began setting children apart from adults. [12]

We set our children apart from practical adult concerns in
many ways. Education, entertainment, and recreation
become peer group activities. Parents find it necessary to
insulate their home life from the pressures and
responsibilities of their work. Even if a trip to the office
does not take forty-five minutes in rush-hour traffic,
parents create a psychological distance between their work
life and their home life. Two hundred years ago this was
not the case; children were involved in their parents' work.
Today, children have little idea of how the real world
operates. Not only that, but children are less aware of how to
deal with people outside of their immediate peer group.
The mobility and mentality of our day has considerably
reduced children's involvement with grandparents and
uncles and aunts. Because "kids are segregated by age" they
are unskilled in the art of caring for both the young and
old. Children development expert, Urie Bronfenbrenner, in
a recent interview said,

In my judgment young people who have never cared for
small children have missed an education in caring. . . .
There's something wrong with this system. . . . We've
moved away from certain traditional family structures
without instituting new ways of doing all the things
families used to do. [13]

Our churches have followed society's example by
dividing the family up into nice, neat, age divisions. We
certainly do not exemplify structurally a family of families.
Instead, we are a collection of peer groups, with each
group, from infants to senior citizens, being molded by the
particular interests and concerns of their secular
counterparts. The local church suffers from the tyranny of
peer group fragmentation. Youthful enthusiasm is not
joined with adult maturity. Singles are denied beneficial
involvement in the lives of families. The aged suffer
alone without the companionship of their sons and
daughters in the Lord.

Removing all age group distinctions would be

over-reacting. However, the present limitations imposed
by our culture need to be reversed *not* reinforced. Children
are caught in a confusing predicament. They are entrusted
with few responsibilities, but are expected to be high
achievers. Bronfenbrenner comments,

Lack of responsibility is a real problem. The inutility of
childhood in America is a striking fact. We don't let our
children do anything important. Maybe they take out the
garbage, but that's it. They're useless because we have
made them useless. They have no experience in being
responsible for other human beings. [14]

Yet today's child shoulders a burden children decades ago
did not have to contend with.

Robert Coles, a child psychiatrist at Harvard, suggests
that due to the decline of religion and increasing affluence
many parents have turned the security and welfare of their
children into a major obsession. Two hundred years ago
the problem facing many children would have been how to
survive, but for today's children, according to Coles, the
problem is "how to make sense of an avalanche of
possessions, opportunities, possibilities—all of which, in
turn generate demands such as no other children have ever
had to face."[15] Coles description of our "obsession" with
children may not be as contemporary as we think. David
observed a similar pattern in Israel. The Psalmist prayed
to the Lord entreating deliverance;

From men of the world, whose portion is in this life; and
whose belly Thou dost fill with Thy treasure; they are
satisfied with children, and leave their abundance to
their babes [Psalms 17:14, NASB].

The majority of today's parents are not indifferent to
their children. Far from it. But the problem is not the
amount of concern as much as it is the *nature* of concern.
There is a tendency among parents to treat their children as
victims of the environment. The child is less than a
person and more like a product. Parental guidance is
displaced by a host of organizations and activities,
usually oriented around the child's peer group. Parents are

managers, organizers, and chauffeurs, rather than fathers and mothers.

One of the major factors in the breakdown of parent-child relationships has been a widespread loss of ethical and moral conviction among parents. Young people are openly reacting against the same moral principles discreetly undermined by their parents. Parents are placed in the awkward position of teaching to their children values that they themselves no longer hold to be true. In a probability sampling of 1,230 American households with one or more children under thirteen, pollster Daniel Yankelovich found that 43 percent of the parents belong to the "New Breed." However the parents' new values of sexual freedom and self-fulfillment were not directly passed on to their children. The study, "The American Family Report: Raising Children in a Changing Society," states,

The children of the New Breed are being taught patriotism, the importance of saving, the need for hard work, respect for authority and that having sex outside marriage is morally wrong, all of which their parents no longer believe themselves. [16]

Our frantic search to find the best possible environment for our children is matched by our unwillingness to be responsible for our children's behavior. Having lost confidence in moral and spiritual values and in his own authority, the parent abdicates his accountability. He fixes the blame for Johnny's delinquency on the "wrong crowd" or poor teachers or the church.

According to Robert Coles, many parents leave no stone unturned in an effort to find some ideal educational environment for their children. We have so mythologized child training that parenting has become a restless quest for some "outside" expertise that will alleviate our own feelings of inability and insecurity. We turn to everyone but to ourselves, refusing to assume, as Coles puts it, "our own sovereignty . . . as human beings who have a right, even an obligation, to hold on to certain ethical propositions, beliefs, standards—even at a sacrifice." [17]

Building a family in the twentieth century is not an easy task. The revolt against knowable standards and true relationships has created a cultural consensus against the Christian family. It is increasingly apparent that God's way for a man and woman, husband and wife, parent and child is truly revolutionary. The family rooted in the love of Christ and the truth of his Word provides the clearest and boldest testimony to a confused and fragmented world. The Christian family should reveal to the world that the way to true freedom is through love, responsibility, and service.

THE REVOLUTIONARY FAMILY

We are challenged by God to "grow" the family. The key to that growth is the centrality of Christ. Jesus used the imagery of the vine, "Abide in Me, and I in you. As the branch cannot bear fruit of itself, unless it abides in the vine, so neither can you, unless you abide in Me" (John 15:4, NASB). The family is both a spiritual and physical entity. To disregard the spiritual dimension is to deny meaning to the biological union of man, woman, and child. A redemptive relationship to Jesus Christ allows the "branch" of human relationships to grow and develop fruitfully. Christ the center, not the source of sentimental feelings and worn-out traditions, but the mainspring of truth and life, is the sole and sufficient means of genuine love and forgiveness. And these are the building materials for God's front-line community, the family. To many readers the challenge to build the family may seem overly idealistic. When the pressures to conform are so great, how can Christians obey the knowable standards and true relationships set forth in God's Word? Securing the family is a wholistic enterprise. Coming to terms with modern man's view of man, work, and materialism are just as important as sexual morality and child discipline. Pat answers and quick solutions do not establish the family. "Growing" the family is a costly task accomplished best when Christ's Lordship is recognized in every area of life.

Let me suggest three important truths that move the idea of growth off the theoretical shelf and into the daily experience of the family.

(1) Growing the family requires a new attitude toward *time*. Everything about the family takes time—from marriage commitment to child development. There are just no shortcuts in cultivating enduring human relationships. Sad to say, in almost everything we do, including raising the family, we have an "overnight mentality." We want to see success instantly and calculate the results immediately. Let there be no doubt that time is one of our dearest possessions, but when it comes to the family, lavish expenditure of time is a must. It takes time and patience to see the positive effects of discipline and to experience open sharing between parents and child. A family time of prayer and Bible study cannot be started on Monday and appreciated as a necessary and vital "routine" by Thursday. There is no perfect time set aside for building the family. When has there ever been a perfect time for sickness, frustrations, pressures, and loneliness? But all these are part of the human experience and how we handle them or let them handle us makes all the difference in building the family.

There may never be a perfect time to do this or that with the kids. It is sad that we let so many opportunities slip past us in the hope that we will find some free time to do what we really think is important. The free time never comes and we plod along, mumbling, "I haven't the time." In her book, *What Is a Family?*, Edith Schaeffer has written,

When people insist on perfection or nothing, they get nothing. When people insist on having what they daydream as a perfect relationship, they will end up having no relationship at all. When people waste the time they could have—by screaming for more—they will have no time at all. The waste of what could be, by demanding what cannot be, is something we all have lived through in certain periods of our lives, but which we need to put behind us with resolve. [19]

Our preoccupation with the immediate moment needs to be replaced with a long-range perspective. Instead of a fixation with the present we need to focus on the generations. When the Lord spoke to Moses and the people of Israel, he was concerned that the second and third generations remain spiritually alive.

Now this is the commandment, the statutes and the judgments which the Lord your God has commanded me to teach you that you might do them in the land where you are going over to possess it, so that you and your son and your grandson might fear the Lord your God, to keep all His statutes and His commandments, which I command you, all the days of your life, and that your days may be prolonged [Deuteronomy 6:1, 2, NASB].

Establishing important priorities today will mean enduring fruit tomorrow. Growing the family is a time-consuming process. It demands the spiritual foresight of people who are willing to live each day in light of eternity. Now is the time to take the responsibilities and privileges of the family seriously.

(2) Growing the family requires *wholistic training*. "Train up a child in the way he should go, even when he is old he will not depart from it" (Proverbs 22:6, NASB). No substitute can be found for true parental guidance. If the home is to be a place of growth it must be a place of learning. Christian fathers and mothers should transcend the difficulties of raising children in a pagan culture. The lack of confidence and "deferred accountability" characteristic of many parents today should not be true of Christian fathers and mothers.

The non-Christian parent is left with the task of making sense out of relativistic cultural norms. Even though the parent may set a fine example, the child is left without a basis for moral behavior. The absence of real truth eventually causes the parental example to crumble. The Christian parent, however, is in the position of living and speaking God's truth to his children. Sunday School and the youth group are good, but not adequate for all of a child's spiritual training. The primary place for learning and applying the Word of God is not the church but the home. The command to train the Israelite children was not given to the priests but to the parents. In Deuteronomy 6, Moses makes special reference to the manner of training to be used by parents:

Hear, O Israel! The Lord is our God, the Lord is one! And you shall love the Lord your God with all your heart and all your soul and with all your might. And these words, which I am commanding you today, shall be on your heart; and you shall teach them diligently to your sons and shall talk of them when you sit in your house and when you walk by the way and when you lie down and when you rise up [Deuteronomy 6:4-7, NASB].

Every possible activity becomes an opportunity for training. To meet this challenge the parent must be filled with a consciousness of the Word of God. This does not mean the parent quotes scriptural truisms every minute of the day, but it does mean that the parent is spiritually alert. Both his mentality and his actions are shaped by the Word of God. The child is faced with the truth of God and not a "holier than thou" attitude. Training which takes place in this manner respects the child as a whole person, with a mind and a unique personality. Children are invited to ask questions and search for meaning.

The Israelite parent was instructed to be sensitive to a child's questions. An adequate response emphasized God's historic and objective work and not the parent's subjective feeling.

When your son asks you in time to come, saying, "What do the testimonies and the statutes and the judgments mean which the Lord commanded you?" then you shall say to your son, "We were slaves to Pharaoh in Egypt; and the Lord brought us from Egypt with a mighty hand. . . ." [Deuteronomy 6:20, 21, NASB].

Wholistic training is necessary for the child's emotional, intellectual, spiritual, and physical maturity. Edith Schaeffer has written,

The family is the place where loyalty, dependability, trustworthiness, compassion, sensitivity to others, thoughtfulness, and unselfishness are supposed to have their roots. Someone must take the initiative and use imagination to intentionally teach these things. [19]

The home is not a prison. It is a proving ground. It is the place where children learn from careful and thoughtful instruction what it means to follow Christ in the daily joys and difficulties of life. The gospel is applied on the primary level of life—in the home where husband and wife, parent and child, brother and sister *learn* to relate to one another through Christ's love.

(3) The growth of the family requires *trust*. Christ does not remove the Christian family from the fallen world. We are subject to the normal pressures and problems of any family. There are also special trials that attack the Christian because he belongs to God and seeks to uphold his truth. The Apostle James wrote,

Consider it all joy, my brethren, when you encounter various trials, knowing that the testing of your faith produces endurance. And let endurance have its perfect result, that you may be perfect and complete, lacking in nothing [James 1:2-4, NASB].

If we take James's advice seriously we will realize that growth is accomplished not in spite of but because of adversity. Attempting to hold the family together by escaping the problems and pressures of the modern world will only end in failure. We must trust the Lord that the circumstances we face are permitted by God for our growth and his glory. Trust in the Lord will not end in disillusionment and despair.

From 1969-1971 my family went through three major operations. My mother underwent major surgery, my father died from cancer following surgery, and I had major surgery for cancer. Such experiences might have broken my family. Instead they proved to be a stimulus to spiritual growth. No one seeks painful and difficult circumstances, but when they do come, they must be faced with a resolute trust in the sovereign wisdom of God.

We learn to trust the Lord not only for difficult circumstances, but also for people. The parent has confidence in the Lord that he will accomplish his purpose in the life of his son or daughter. Parental training develops within the child a consciousness of God's personal leading. This means, of course, that God may lead a child toward a career and ministry unanticipated by parents. Last year I had a student in my class who had accepted Christ in his late teens. His father had prayed for his conversion for many years but when it finally came it meant changes in the teenager's life the father was reluctant to go along with. He had expected his son to take over his farm, but instead his son believed God was leading him to a Bible College. Conflicts can be avoided by parents and children mutually trusting the Lord. Having been nurtured under the parent's authority and accountability, the child must develop and be allowed to develop a personal sense of responsibility toward God.

If the parent trusts that God is at work in the life of his child, how much more should the child be aware of God's direction in the lives of his parents. Often a young person is given the impression that God's leading is especially needed when it comes to selecting a college or looking for work. Once these big decisions are made, life is smooth sailing until someone becomes sick. But the opposite of this should be true. Trust and dependence upon God deepen as we mature in our relationship to God. Children need the example of parents whose trust in God is continuously real, affecting every area of life.

The growth of a Christian family is certainly no "part-time" job. The family can only be what God intended it to be when parents and children are willing to commit themselves to Christ's Lordship. The result will be a family quite different from what is becoming standard in our modern culture. Edith Schaeffer likens what is happening to today's family to the tragedy of slavery.

But the staggering thing in the twentieth century is the abandonment of responsibility to keep a family together, on the very part of the two adults whose family it is. What a hue and cry there would be today if men and women were

put on a block and auctioned off, leaving behind
weeping babies and children in the split which would be
taking place as they were carted off to two different
geographic locations! . . . Homes of today—shattered and
split as thoroughly as any in slave-auctioning times—by
cold choice.[20]

Regardless of human suffering and societal breakdown,
cultural forces against the family are gaining momentum.
On the basis of God's love and truth, Christians are
called to build a truly revolutionary family. They are
entrusted with the privilege and responsibility of securing
the family. Joshua's pledge has never been more
appropriate: "As for me and my house, we will serve the
Lord" (Joshua 24:15, NASB).

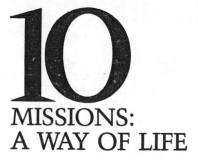

10
MISSIONS:
A WAY OF LIFE

Archbishop William Temple once said, "The Church is the only society in the world which exists for the benefit of those who do not belong to it." His statement does not say everything there is to say about the Church, but it does underscore the mission of Christ's body. There is little use in grappling with Christ's claim upon our lives in the twentieth century if we are not convinced that Christ has entrusted the Church with a mission. We are not saved by Almighty God in order to be contented churchgoers. If that were the case, what we have been talking about now has little relevance.

Shortly before Jesus was crucified he made it very clear to the disciples that he had called them out of the world. His prayer to the Father reveals their new identity and their new responsibility.

I have given them Thy word; and the world has hated them, because they are not of the world. . . . I do not ask Thee to take them out of the world, but to keep them from the evil one. They are not of the world, even as I am not of the world. Sanctify them in the truth; Thy word is truth. As Thou didst send Me into the world, I also have sent them into the world [John 17:14-18, NASB].

The "sentness" of Christ results in the "sentness" of the believer. In as much as Christ's humanity was essential for our redemption, our transformed humanity is essential for our mission. Christ "emptied himself, taking the form of a bondservant, and being found in appearance as a man, He humbled himself by becoming obedient to the point of death, even death on a cross" (Philippians 2:7, 8, NASB). Sent by the Father, Christ confronted culture. His message was singular and wholistic. Through his life, death, and resurrection he revealed to man that the only way of salvation was by a life commitment to the incarnate Son of God. His finished work gave rise to the divinely appointed task of the Church.

We must never forget that "the living God of the Bible is a sending God."[1] He called us out of the world in order to send us back into the world. The stakes could not be higher. What is at issue is not our personal peace and security, but the believability of Jesus Christ. Think of it! Christ has entrusted to us the testimony of his Lordship. Whether or not the world believes in Jesus is decided by our faithfulness or faithlessness.

I do not ask in behalf of these alone, but for those also who believe in Me through their word; that they may all be one; even as Thou, Father, art in Me, and I in Thee, that they also may be in Us; that the world may believe that Thou didst send Me. And the glory which Thou hast given Me I have given to them; that they may be one, just as We are one; I in them, and Thou in Me, that they may be perfected in unity, that the world may know that Thou didst send Me, and didst love them, even as Thou didst love Me [John 17:20, 21, NASB].

Can life hold a more privileged purpose than to manifest Jesus Christ? Is this not sufficient motivation to transform our way of life through the power of the Holy Spirit? If we are truly Christ's followers, the watching world is bound to discern, quite often antagonistically, the change Christ has made in our lives. This wholistic change, affecting the totality of our lives, from our deepest intellectual convictions and emotional commitment to our daily interaction with others and our attitude toward possessions, is essential to the Christian's mission.

The "sentness" of the believer encompasses a world as intimate as the home and as far-reaching as the nations. It is a world as near as your neighbor and as far as God's love. The very domain of Satan, the Prince of this world, is the proving ground of the gospel. The Christian is sent by Christ across the wastelands of modern culture and the frontiers of primitive cultures with a message of deliverance. As the recipients of both the Great Commission, "Go and make disciples," and the Great Commandment, "Love your neighbor," believers are called forth to courageously and compassionately confront their culture.

There are three common rationalizations that stand in the way of our faithful acceptance of the Christian mission.

1. *A Diminished Gospel.* In an earlier chapter dealing with the social implications of the gospel, I discussed our callousness to man's wholistic needs and our tendency to emphasize a personal faith commitment to Christ without showing a compassionate sacrificial love for man's physical needs. The North American church has taught many Third World believers that the demands of the gospel upon our life-style are nonexistent. The result has been a weak and shallow view of what it means to follow Jesus. In the words of Dietrich Bonhoeffer, we have turned God's "costly grace" into "cheap grace."

Cheap grace is grace without discipleship, grace without the cross, grace without Jesus Christ, living and incarnate. . . . Grace is costly because it calls us to follow and it is grace because it calls us to follow Jesus Christ. It is costly because it costs a man his life, and it is grace because it gives a man the only true life. It is costly because it condemns sins, and grace because it justifies the sinner. Above all, it is costly because it cost God the life of his Son: "ye were bought at a price" and what has cost God much cannot be cheap to us.[2]

We cannot divide up the gospel and choose doctrine over practice, or practice over doctrine. Truth and action cannot be divorced. To disregard either one is to deny both. It is not a matter of choosing either evangelism or

social action. The Christian mission involves both
evangelism and social action. If you have one you must have
the other. If God sends us with the complete gospel for
the whole man, how dissatisfied he must be when we
present a partial gospel to a modular man. A diminished
gospel belongs to a declining Church. It engenders neither
motivation nor sacrifice.

2. *Specialized Personnel.* A great failure in the Church
today has been the tendency to consider the Christian
mission as a *speciality* of the church's operation.
Involvement in this task is limited to those who experience
a special "call" to become missionaries. Louis Luzbetak
points up a difference between today's prevailing attitude
and the outlook of the early church:

*In the early Church missionary activities were not
regarded as a form of specialization: to be a Christian
was to be a missionary, a spirit that prevailed during the
first five centuries of the Christian era. The subsequent
channelization of apostolic interests into a specialized
group tended to make apostolic interests accidental to
Christianity. . . . Nothing could be more detrimental to the
apostolic cause; the more or less exclusive concern of
specialists called "missionaries."*[3]

Responsibility for the mission of the Church is as real to
each and every believer as the forgiveness of sin. No believer
is more "called" than another believer. All believers are
"called out" and "sent back"; all are "ambassadors" for
Christ. The difference is not between those who have
received a call and those who have not. The difference is
between those who have been obedient to the call and
those who have been disobedient. The entire Church is
called to self-denial and sacrifice, not just a small handful
of men and women. The rise of the "professional" Christian
worker in the ranks of the Church has made some
believers feel less accountable to Christ's commands. To
excuse our withdrawal from front-line evangelism and
social action we have raised salaries, built seminaries, and
listened to conference speakers. Such efforts are

commendable, but not if they reduce our sense of responsibility for the mission of the Church.

The necessary division of labor in the Church does not eliminate each believer's responsibility. In order to meet the full spectrum of man's physical and spiritual needs, the responsibility must be shared and the specific tasks coordinated through the Church. This was done in Acts 6 when the Apostles advised the Church to select "seven men of good reputation, full of the Spirit and of wisdom." Their duties were to make certain that all, especially the widows, received ample provision. Another example of this division of labor can be found in Acts 13. Moved by the Holy Spirit, the Church at Antioch "set apart" Paul and Barnabas for the "overseas" work God had called them to perform. From its earliest days the Church has adhered to a division of labor, with each member of the body expected to function according to the gifts he or she had received from God.

For just as we have many members in one body and all the members do not have the same function, so we, who are many, are one body in Christ, and individually members one of another. And since we have gifts that differ according to the grace given to us, let each exercise them accordingly. . . . [Romans 12:4-6, NASB].

The Christian mission cannot be delegated a second time. God has commissioned us all in a task of tremendous magnitude. We cannot delegate our responsibility to another believer. It is our cross to bear. The Bible says, "He who does not take his cross and follow after Me is not worthy of Me" (Matthew 10:38, NASB). In his wisdom, God has seen fit to "set apart" some men and women for a special task. Not all Christians are either gifted or appointed to be pastors or "professional" missionaries. Not all the God-fearing Israelites in Elijah's day were called to be prophets, but all were called to be representatives of God's distinctive minority. The Bible tells us that 7,000 stood with Elijah against Baal; obviously not all were prophets, but all were God's called out people (1 Kings 19:18). God individually calls us to different tasks, and he uses a variety

of means to make each specific task and course of life
known to us. However, the responsibility for the Christian
mission is the shared concern of all Christians. In fact,
the specially trained, church-supported missionary and the
businessman are equally responsible for upholding
Christ's name in a pagan culture, be it primitive or modern.

3. *Restricted Mission.* "Go and make disciples" is not
limited to a small group of professionals, and neither is it
restricted to a "foreign field." We tend to interpret the
mission of the Church as a vague endeavor taking place
"somewhere else." The early Church was instructed to
begin their witness in the immediate surroundings of
Jerusalem. This meant that no part of their daily lives was
removed from the transforming impact of Jesus Christ.

"Go and make disciples" did not mean placing a certain
geographical distance between their spiritual ministry
and the real world of their family, friends, work, and
cultural customs. What was true then is true today. The
"sentness" of the believer results in a front-line cultural
confrontation wherever he or she may be.

At no point is a culture completely Christian. Even in
areas "saturated" by professing believers and large
churches, the forces mitigating against a truly Christian
life-style are great. The appearance of a Christian cultural
consensus is quite often deceiving. In the very place where
we would expect the Church to be its strongest because
of a large number of Christians, abundant material
resources, educational opportunities, and a great variety
of spiritual gifts, the Church is often weak and indifferent.
The first indication of declining participation in world
missions is spiritual complacency in the "home" culture.
When Christians are indistinguishable from the main
stream of culture, their interest in missions becomes a
traditional duty or a polite gesture of support for the
"full-time Christian worker." The same believers who
radically apply the Word of God in their "native" culture
are the believers vitally concerned with the proclamation
of the gospel in other countries. As long as the gospel
mission is restricted to the "never, never land of somewhere

else" our attitude toward world missions will be impersonal and indifferent. The commands of Jesus to "go and make disciples" and to "love your neighbor" are clearly meant to be obeyed here and now.

The vastness and intimacy of the scope of Christian missions means that the gospel cannot be "tied down" to purely local characteristics. If Jesus Christ is truly the incarnate Son of God and man's only hope for salvation, the gospel message must remain free from cultural attachments that discredit its universality. Inherent in God's truth is an inclusiveness that defies cultural barriers. The "sent" Christian is a "global" Christian. He realizes that the order of his worship, the manner of his teaching, the style of his music, the building in which he worships, the time he reserves for prayer, the way he helps his neighbor, and the "method" of his witness are all expressions of his local culture. But he is also aware that to worship, to teach, to praise, to pray, to minister, and to witness is to join with believers worldwide in their obedience to the commands of God. Christianity is not steepled churches, stained-glass windows, and polished pews. It is the living Lord Jesus, our Savior and Redeemer.

Although the forms we use to express this truth are not insignificant, we must be careful not to compromise the truth by making our cultural forms equal to the truth or challenging to the spirituality of one who expresses his faith in Christ in a manner to which we are not accustomed. Inflexible and inappropriate forms can become a problem in any culture. A thorough and careful study of the Word of God increases our ability to discern between God's truth and cultural forms.

Besides the confusion of form and truth, another obstacle the "global" Christian must hurdle is the opinion among many peoples that Christianity is part and parcel of the Western World. In their view, the cultural religion of the materialistically successful, media-conditioned North American just happens to be Christianity. Other cultures, under the pretense of maintaining their traditional ideological commitment, swallow whole the naturalistic world and life view of the Western World. This is especially evident in the East. Developing nations accept the West's technological philosophy of life, but often reject in whole or in part the West's pseudo-religious commitment. The most frequent objection against Christianity that I heard during my teaching year in Taiwan was that it represented a cultural religion on the same level as Taoism or Buddhism. My students saw their eclectic Eastern religions as a fitting counterpart to my faith in Christ. For some of them, opposition to Christianity meant a "last stand" resistance against Western ideological domination.

The early Church had to free itself from Jewish provincialism. The universality of the gospel message was threatened by those who wished to restrict outreach to the Jews and life-style to Jewish forms. Likewise, the twentieth-century believer is responsible for freeing the Church from the stranglehold of the modern Western mentality. It is the will of God that brothers from the East and from the West commune together in worship and service. All Christians must sacrifice their cultural provincialism for the sake of their Lord. At a time when the North American church suffers from a complacency and indifference wrought by materialism and the Third World church suffers from a prejudicial and often hostile nationalism, we need to be reminded that we are global Christians with a universal gospel: "One Lord, one faith, one baptism."

If I tell you that my skin color is white, my language English, that I have a college education, and that I carry an American passport, I have told you something about my "label." Obviously, the Chinese engineering student, living in a small Taiwan village with a Taoist background is going to have a different cultural label. But regardless of these "labels" our identity is the same because of our personal commitment to Jesus Christ. Paul Rees of World Vision has written,

Centrally, the Christian mission in the world is not a matter of geography but of identity—knowing who I am as a person in Christ and a person in a community of persons who also are in Christ.[4]

TRANSFERABLE PRINCIPLES
FOR THE "GLOBAL" CHRISTIAN

There is a great deal that the "overseas" missionary can teach us about sharing the gospel with modern, twentieth-century man. With the help of God, the foreign missionary has bridged the culture gulf, and God, by means of the missionary, has established his Church. The seemingly insurmountable cultural barriers have been transcended by the sacrificial and penetrating love of Christ. More often than not, the missionary has approached a foreign culture with sensitivity, patience, and wisdom. Practically, this has meant that the missionary abides by three important principles. First, he must genuinely identify with the people. Second, he must find an appropriate starting point from which to share the gospel. Third, he must train new disciples to preserve the purity of the gospel. As we look at these three principles we will see how important they are for carrying out the Christian mission in our modern culture.

1. *Developing Empathy.* The first step toward effective communication of the gospel is understanding the people and their culture. Louis Luzbetak writes,

A missionary with true empathy views all native ways and values not through his colored glasses known as "enculturation" but in full native context. Without approving polygamy the missionary must understand why his people are polygamists, and without tolerating fetishism or promiscuity he must understand why his people venerate fetishes and are promiscuous. Empathy means that I understand why my people are what they are no matter what they are. Although empathy is internal, it is nonetheless clearly perceptible to the local people, and it is a prerequisite for genuine apostolic identification. [5]

If the missionary thought only of his own contentment and pleasure, he would never develop an understanding of the people. In a foreign situation, cultivating empathy is not an easy task. It takes "violence to self" to adapt to everyday customs, from eating habits and hygiene to the rules of etiquette.

Many missionaries experience culture shock in various degrees. Missionaries can "crack" under the psychological and emotional strain of adjusting to a new culture. According to Luzbetak, extreme culture shock can be manifested in two ways. The individual may develop a deep-seated resentment of anything and everything that suggests the "native" culture. Accompanying this disdain for the foreign environment is an obsession for the missionary's home culture. Unless he is in the company of a Westerner and eating American food, he is depressed and miserable.

A completely opposite culture shock reaction is the passionate desire to find security by "going native." He rejects his "home" culture and attempts to copy the foreign culture right down to the smallest peculiarity. Luzbetak writes,

"Going Native" . . . is not apostolic; rather, it is a neurotic longing for security and an exaggerated hunger for belonging. This unbalanced craving for acceptance drives the unwary individual to approve and to accept as his own, indiscriminately and blindly, any and all local ways and values.[6]

The difference between empathy and culture shock is the difference between self-denial and self-inflicted pain. Empathy is costly, but it is the only way to meaningful and joyful service. Just as costly, but in a destructive sense, is unchecked culture shock. It is the surest way to ruin a potentially effective ministry.

Neither the values of empathy nor the problems of culture shock are limited to the so-called foreign field. We deal with both on a day-to-day basis in our own culture. One of the purposes of this book has been to develop a deeper understanding of the modern Western culture. We may not have to learn a language and adjust to a new diet, but we do have to know what lies beneath the veneer of the modern twentieth-century culture. In order for us to penetrate our culture with the gospel, we must be willing to understand our culture and empathize with its people. Jesus did not condone the sin of Zaccheus and the religiosity of Nicodemus. He did not run from the Gerasene demoniac or shrink from judging the Pharisees. Jesus knew the people he was dealing with (John 2:25). Each of his encounters reveals an awareness of the cultural and spiritual forces shaping the life of the individual. Jesus was not a victim of culture shock. Normally, a Galilean would have been out of place debating with Jerusalem scribes, or conversing with a Samaritan woman, or standing before the Roman governor, but Jesus was not. His understanding of all men made authentic communication possible.

Christ-like empathy is available to us through the Holy Spirit. He enables us to be spiritually and culturally discerning and to apply the truth of God's Word in the cultural context. The presence of God's Spirit, however, does not make empathy automatic nor does it eliminate self-denial. It may take a great deal of patience and sacrificial love before you or I can truly empathize with our neighbors. The overseas missionary is not the only one who must struggle for a genuine understanding of the people he desires to reach for Christ. It is a requirement of *all* believers and becoming increasingly more difficult in the fragmented Western culture. Without knowing it, we are often victims of culture shock. Through withdrawal or conformity, we isolate ourselves from the very people Christ has sent us to reach. We must be careful not to be so repulsed or threatened by immorality and broken families that we fail to minister to needy people or so attracted to our affluent life-style that we make the gospel secondary.

2. *Finding a Starting Point.* Closely related to the need for empathy is the importance of discovering appropriate ways to share the gospel effectively. Louis Luzbetak has written,

The thought-process may be the same for all human beings, but the actual starting point in reasoning will differ from culture to culture. . . . To arrive at the mentality of his people, the missionary will have to

*discover their basic premises, their underlying
assumptions, or postulates, otherwise effective
communication will be impossible.* [7]

When John the Baptist cried out, "Behold the Lamb of God!"
he introduced Jesus in a very appropriate manner. Because
of their Old Testament heritage, the Jews attributed a great
deal of significance to the sacrificial lamb. By using the
imagery of the lamb, John made the truth of Jesus
immediately relevant and thought-provoking for his
listeners. The Apostle Paul did much the same thing when
he addressed the Athenians.

*For while I was passing through and examining the objects
of your worship, I also found an altar with this
inscription, "TO AN UNKNOWN GOD." What therefore
you worship in ignorance, this I proclaim to you. . .*
[Acts 17:23, NASB].

The account in Acts tells us that Paul was provoked at the
idolatry of the Athenians. But instead of going off in a
huff—condemning those foolish Athenians—he actually
used one of their idols as a "starting point" for effective
gospel proclamation. Throughout the Bible we see
numerous instances where the truth of God is introduced
in a way which especially suits the immediate cultural
context. Truth does not change from culture to culture, but
people's thought processes do.

   Don Richardson describes in *Peace Child* his attempts to
penetrate for Christ the culture of the Sawi Indians in New
Guinea. After months of living with the Indians and
learning their language and customs he was frustrated
with his inability to communicate the gospel. In fact, the
more he learned about their customs the more difficult
the task of presenting the gospel appeared to be.

*. . . we found that we were living and working among a
people who honor treachery as an ideal. In many of the
legends that the Sawi people tell to their children
around the campfires the heroes are men who formed
friendship with the express purpose of later betraying the
befriended one to be killed and eaten. The Sawi expression*

for this practice is "to fatten with friendship for the slaughter."[8]

The breakthrough came quite unexpectedly. Don was convinced that his presence had drawn together into one community two Sawi tribes. The close proximity of the tribes served to intensify their hatred for another, making it only a matter of time before all-out fighting began. In order to alleviate the growing pressure toward violence, Don told the leaders of each tribe that he would move away in order to encourage the tribes to separate. Much to his surprise the leaders responded with a peace proposal. But in a culture where treachery was idealized, Don questioned how a genuine peace was possible. He never imagined that this "peace" would offer a cultural "starting point" for presenting the gospel.

The next day Don discovered the one custom in the Sawi tribe that took precedence over their ideal of treachery. Each tribe proved their sincerity for peace by offering to the other tribe a "peace-child." This meant that one family from each tribe sacrificially gave up their own son in order to ensure peace for the entire tribe. As long as the two children remained alive the tribes were bound to their peace agreement. This was the starting point that Don and Carol Richardson had prayed for. Don writes,

The key God gave us to the heart of the Sawi people was the principle of redemptive analogy—the application to local custom of spiritual truth. The principle we discerned was that God had already provided for the evangelization of these people by means of redemptive analogies in their own culture. These analogies were our stepping-stones, the secret entryway by which the gospel came into the Sawi culture and started both a spiritual and a social revolution from within.[9]

Finding an appropriate "starting point" is as necessary for the believer living in the West as it was for Don Richardson living with the Sawi Indians. The Christian mission cannot be fulfilled apart from a Spirit-led sensitivity to the world views of modern men and women. God's grace was meant to take a man from where he is as a sinner to where God chooses him to be as a disciple. The road of transformation begins with a clear and convicting word—a universal message intended by God to be as personal and meaningful in one culture as another.

3. *Guarding the Purity of the Gospel.* The discovery and use of meaningful cultural "bridges" to make the gospel known is only the beginning. True conversion involves an integration of the gospel in culture. No area of life can be rightfully excluded from the all embracing demands of the Lordship of Jesus Christ. "The truth is," writes Eugene Nida, "if God is left out of anything, He is not entirely in anything."[10] Applying the message of Christ calls for true spiritual leadership. When new converts are allowed to select which commands are to be obeyed and which should be ignored, the gospel suffers serious distortion. On the other hand, if the gospel is applied wholistically, a believer's way of life is bound to change. Something has to change—either the gospel's integrity or the culture's domination. True communication of the gospel means that the missionary must know both the Word of God and the culture well enough to integrate the gospel without compromise. Louis Luzbetak has written,

The process of integration must be so directed that the Good News remains theologically sound both in substance as well as in emphasis. Not what the local people prefer but what happens to be the true content of the Christian Message is the object of cultural integration, and the various items of that content must at all times retain their theologically defined propositions. . . . Nothing invites syncretism to develop more than letting the likes and dislikes of a new Christian community rather than sound theology decide the content and emphasis of the missionary message.[11]

Anglican Bishop Stephen Neill reminds us, "We cannot evade the fact that Christ is Destroyer as well as Savior. When he comes in, certain things have to go."[12] The popular notion today is that missionaries are aggressive

Westerners intent on destroying tribal customs and treading down the races. They are accused of exploiting instead of ministering. Stephen Neill calls this notion "mythology." "The fact is," says Neill, "that missionaries do more than anybody else to preserve the structures of these people's lives."[13]

In an interview with *Christianity Today*, Rachel Saint, missionary to the Auca Indians in Ecuador, was asked her response to the criticism that missionaries destroy primitive cultures.

I have thought about it a great deal and I have come to the conclusion that we are actually giving the Indians back that which they lost, maybe hundreds of years ago. In the stories of the Indians, they recognize one God. They do not know his Son, nor his name. But they have many of the stories that seem to be universal among primitive peoples, stories of the flood, of the personal dealing of God with men. So we are simply taking them back to their old, old stories and filling in the facts of the Gospel. We really are giving them the conclusion of their own culture, not robbing them of something pure and innocent.[14]

In spite of Paul's apostolic ministry, the Galatians became selective in their application of biblical truth. Popular opinion began to shape the Church and distort the gospel, making it necessary for Paul to write to the Galatians,

I am amazed that you are so quickly deserting Him who called you by the grace of Christ, for a different gospel; which is really not another; only there are some who are disturbing you, and want to distort the gospel of Christ [Galatians 1:6, 7, NASB].

Looking back on the Galatian situation with the help of Paul's letter, it is not difficult for us to see the problem. But does *their* situation make us more sensitive to the ways *we* compromise the gospel? Often we can recognize the problem of syncretism in other cultures better than our own: for example, the North American Indian who professes faith in Christ, but thinks of baptism as nothing more than a form of magic, or the young Chinese convert who continues faithfully to practice ancestor worship.

Distorting the gospel is not limited to foreign cultures. As we have seen earlier, our culture exerts a tremendous influence upon our lives.

Our intensive preoccupation with self is one example of how our culture affects our application of biblical truth. We are culturally conditioned to think first of our rights and pleasures and to interpret God's Word in terms of self-fulfillment and self-identity. Recently a believer from Ghana shared with me how he had interrupted his education in Africa to work for a year. Of course there's nothing very unusual about taking a year off to earn some money—many North American students do it all the time. But the reason he gave me for working is almost unheard of in our culture. He went to work for a year to support an older, more mature believer who was finishing his last year of Bible school training. What we might deem as a rare instance of personal sacrifice, my African Christian brother perceived to be a natural and practical offering to the Lord and his African coworker.

In a variety of ways, from interpersonal relationships and methods of communication to materialism and education, there is a subtle and often not so subtle pressure to modify and compromise the gospel. It is the responsibility of all believers to guard the gospel. Whether our native culture is Sawi, Brazilian, Canadian, or American, it is imperative that we preserve the gospel's purity and integrate it completely.

Wherever there are men and women in need of Christ, there are cultural frontiers to be crossed. Learning a new language and adapting to new customs may or may not be required. Like Ezekiel, we may be called to our "home" culture.

Son of man, go to the house of Israel and speak with My words to them. For you are not being sent to a people of unintelligible speech or difficult language, but to the house of Israel. . . . to them who should listen to you [Ezekiel 3:4-6, NASB].

Even though he was a native Israelite, Ezekiel did not find it easy penetrating the spiritual and cultural frontier with the Word of God. God demanded of him a costly way of life that lived out God's message to the people. Are we prepared to invest our lives in proclaiming Christ's gospel? Are we mindful that there are still cultures today where Jesus' question, "Who do you say that I am?" has never been introduced and many other cultures where it has been silenced or distorted? To follow Christ is to be a missionary in the fullest sense of the word. Whether God has called you to labor for him at "home" or "abroad," the harvest is ready for the "global" Christian.

11
THE NEW REFORMATION

In this book we have dealt with a number of important aspects involved in the relationship between the Christian and the modern culture. We have not dealt with all of the issues involved, but those we have covered are intended to deepen our insight into our culture and strengthen our commitment to Jesus Christ. Reading alone does not bring spiritual maturity, but applying the Word of God does. It is not enough for us to become expert diagnosticians while remaining weak and ineffective Christians. Proclaiming the victory of Christ and remaining a victim of culture will not do. We must do more than acknowledge the pressures opposing a Christian life-style. True understanding involves Christ-centered confrontation with cultural conformity. The way of Christ is against the way of Satan and the world. Coming to terms with modern man means far more than a critical look at the disintegrating family, the manipulating media, or the problems of materialism. In essence, spiritual reformation means coming to terms with the Lord Jesus Christ in the practical, daily situation. There are three important truths that will help to conceptualize what we have studied in the previous chapters: culture is a matter of the mind, culture is the "adaptive system," and culture is the place for integration.

1. *Culture Is a Matter of the Mind.* If anyone claims the critical importance of the mind, it ought to be the Christian. In our study we have seen how the twentieth-century mentality has deeply influenced our daily actions. Culture is the product of man's thoughts. The proverb is true, "as a man thinketh so is he." Culture gives to us an interpretative framework, a reference point from which to determine the mind of man. The importance of the mind does not apply to only university professors, business leaders, or authors. We are all actively engaged in communicating what is on our mind. Culture does for humanity what words do for ideas. It is the painter's canvas, the sculptor's clay, the musician's score. It is a vehicle for expressing the thoughts and intents of man's heart. As in human language, culture is filled with a confusing array of voices. On the surface it would appear impossible to derive a singular message. It may be argued that to arrive at the "modern mentality" would be as impossible as summarizing on a single page all the volumes in a university library. But the diversity in thought and cultural expression which is all around us can be judged by another interpretative framework, namely, the Word of God. When the mind of God evaluates the mind of man, the innumerable hopes and perspectives of culture sink into one dilemma—the lostness of man. Our culture is a product of man's Fall. It is rich in beauty and goodness because man is made in God's image, but it is also twisted and broken because man has turned away from God. A host of world views will not change this fact. On every cultural front the conclusion is the same: man is lost and in need of God: "Professing to be wise, they became fools" [Romans 1:22, NASB].

When the Apostle Paul wrote, "Be not conformed to this world: but be ye transformed by the renewing of your mind," he was not encouraging a change in one's religious affiliation or an amendment to one's world and life view. He was calling for a total life transformation. Conformity ceased when life was revolutionized by the mind of Christ. If we are to apply the Word of God, we must first allow our minds and hearts to be molded by God's

revelation. The Word of God must become so deeply
ingrained in our thought processes that our perspective
toward culture corresponds to the mind of Christ. Instead of
profaning the gospel through compromise or
complacency, we will know the will of God. We will know
how to "grow" our families, demonstrate compassion,
use our money, and honestly communicate the gospel of
Christ. What we are talking about is a process of spiritual
development whereby the believer and his local church
become increasingly more aware of the Lordship of
Christ and the culture which surrounds them.

The application of God's Word calls for a prayerful and
disciplined mind. It calls for a man or woman who is
willing to take seriously the divine revelation. The
choice between the broad way and the narrow way is a
choice between the mind of man and the mind of Christ.
It is a choice between the voice of this world and the voice
of Christ. There can be no ultimate duality of allegiance.
Either the mind of Christ progressively applies the Word of
God in our lives or the mind of man aggressively
conforms our lives into the way of the world.

The new mentality is actually a new way of living. It
causes us to rethink our position in culture in light of the
one true reference point—the living Lord Jesus. As our
understanding of him deepens, all of life is brought into
focus.

2. *Culture Is the "Adaptive System."* In this study we have
isolated specific areas of culture and dealt with these topics
individually. It is my hope that this has clarified in a
practical way what it means to follow Jesus Christ in our
contemporary culture. The confrontation between a
Christ-centered Christian and his surrounding culture is
well beyond a theologian's abstractions. Discipleship is
always on the immediate level of life's daily tasks. Therefore
we must be careful to add here that culture cannot be
divided up in any realistic way. Come Monday morning, no
single part of culture can remain independent from the rest
of culture. When we talk about culture, we are talking about
a pervasive, interrelated system, an embracing totality

resembling a tangled knot of many strands.

Ever since Adam sinned against God, man has been in the business of shaping his way of life around a fallen world. Culture is man's way of being successful. It is his attempt to cope with an environment permeated by sin. However, man's vantage point is strictly one-dimensional. He weaves his cultural web irrespective of God's revelation. In many cases we have seen that the most expedient means for cultural "success" is sin itself. The contemporary solution for the problem of separation between God and man is idolatry. Preeminent in our minds and in our culture are the idols of materialism, self-gratification, and a naturalistic world and life view. The separation between man and man is resolved by modular relationships, sexual immorality, and media manipulation. It is readily apparent that the manner in which man attempts to deal with his situation only serves to intensify his despair. He lies at the mercy of the very system he is responsible for creating.

The momentum of the "adaptive system" moves man further and further away from the knowledge of God and obedience to his will. Satan is an "expert applied anthropologist."[1] He knows the nature of culture and that man is a creature of culture. His work goes on undetected in the cultural milieu, perpetuated and intensified with each passing generation. This is easy for us to see in countries governed by communism. A whole generation has grown up as far removed as possible from the gospel of Christ. In communism Satan has engineered a way of life diametrically opposed to Christianity. But Satan's impact is hardly limited to places where the freedom of worship is restricted, Christians are persecuted, and Bibles are contraband. The brazenness of communism parallels the subtlety of Western culture. Satan achieves the same demoniac goal in our Western culture, as much through moral and ethical relativism, the possessiveness of affluence, and the disintegrating family as through blatant aggression against the Church.

It is important for the believer to understand the growing cultural consensus against Christianity and that the momentum of culture is an instrument in Satan's use for perpetuating man's separation from God. Our Western society has all but lost the conviction of God's ordained absolutes. We are living today in the post-Christian era, not because there are fewer Christians, but because men and women have rejected the principles that were once accepted as God-given truths applicable for all men, believers and non-believers alike. The result has been the development of a cultural consensus which makes the "Christian West" as resistant to the gospel as the Orient or the Islamic nations. In many ways, our culture is under the wrath of God. We have seen it in the family, in business, in the media, and in inter-personal relationships.

In the first chapter of Paul's Epistle to the Romans we read that the wrath of God is revealed "against all ungodliness and unrighteousness of men, who suppress the truth in unrighteousness." Three times the phrase is repeated, "God gave them up" to impurity, to degrading passions, and to a depraved mind. Likewise, God has given up our culture to the conclusion of its own sinfulness.

Put on the full armor of God, that you may be able to stand firm against the schemes of the devil [Ephesians 6:11, NASB].

Confronting our culture with the good news of Jesus Christ is a total life commitment. As the Spirit of God applies the revealed Word of God to our lives, we must be willing, in the power and wisdom of God, to act accordingly. All that is of Christ transforms our behavior in the whole of culture. "In the world but not of the world" is pushed to its ultimate limit. All of life becomes the proving ground of the gospel.

I believe it is significant that the world chose to identify the early Church simply as "The Way." Although the designation was apparently conceived by the world, it was nevertheless appropriate. It captures in a word the Church's singular devotion to Jesus Christ. Even the world perceived that the body of Christ could not be relegated to a religious, social, or ethnic sphere. Here was a community which confronted the whole of culture because it embraced the crucified and risen Christ. The early believers knew they were engaged in a spiritual struggle. The lines of confrontation were drawn between the way of the world and the way of Christ.

3. Culture Is the Place for Integration.

I do not ask Thee to take them out of the world, but to keep them from the evil one. They are not of the world, even as I am not of the world [John 17:15, 16, NASB].

We are not concerned with reshaping the "adaptive system"—hoping to make people who are not Christians act like Christians. We are concerned with implementing Christian values in the whole of society, but we must always bear in mind the necessity of a wholistic spiritual transformation in each person's life if these values are to be internalized. At the heart of the gospel is the message of redemption and the forgiveness of sin. Jesus Christ lived and died and rose again to restore individuals to their proper fellowship with God. This is the bedrock truth upon which all other relationships and issues must rest. The outer man is changed because the inner man has found true peace with God through Jesus Christ. However, to "Christianize" society is to circumvent the need for spiritual transformation. Many people know enough about Christ to be uncomfortable with culture, but they have not come to Christ to be transformed by him in culture. "Christianization" settles for maintaining the status quo or calling for a return to past traditions.

The life-style of the church is usually one step behind the current cultural trends. The only apparent difference between the church and culture is that the church is the last bastion of conservatism to give in to change. "Christianizing" society is well suited to the interests of nominal Christianity. The church represents culture's highest ideals. Its people are enlightened and pragmatic, wanting the best for themselves and their culture. The church of culture only affirms the adaptive system; it does not transform it. It is a small voice in a chorus of cultural consent. Jacques Ellul writes,

What does man expect?—quite simply that the Church, speaking for God, should tell man that he is right—quite

simply that one should proclaim "Jesus' faith in man." In that case man can calmly go back to his business and act as he sees fit! In his eyes the Church is there to provide him with justification, but not of course, the justification which Jesus Christ provides![1]

The world negates the gospel when it makes the church like itself. In the church's attempt to shape society it has drifted so far from Christ that to confront culture would be to confront itself. A church *of* culture has no business being *in* culture.

The true believer stands as a distinctive minority, integrating the exclusive and timeless claims of Christ in a changing culture. He is not passive or compromising in his declaration of the truth. His special concern is not with the adaptive system but with individual men and women and children who need personally to know Jesus Christ. The Christian increases his impact upon culture by authentically substantiating his words with "Thus saith the Lord." He lives as a Jeremiah or an Elijah willing to confront the world with the sure Word of God. His position on abortion, drugs, trade relations, human rights, and sexual morality may not suit the enlightened ideal of the conforming church. But he is willing to speak his mind, affirming that the ultimate validity for biblical propositions is in the person of God and that the way to truth and life is through Jesus Christ.

The Church of Christ is a called-out minority directed toward the cultural majority. Neither withdrawal nor accommodation are valid options. For the glory of Christ and out of compassion for man, the Christian enters the cultural arena. He does not turn to the world for an agenda. His ministry and his message are appointed by Christ. The fundamental issue is God's question to man, not man's questions about God. Dr. Visser't Hooft has written,

I do not believe that evangelism is adequately described as answering the questions which men are asking, however deep those questions may be. For evangelism is in the first place the transmission of God's question to man. And that question is and remains whether we are willing to accept Christ as the one and only Lord of life.[2]

Culture does not confront Christ. Christ confronts culture. The non-negotiable revelation of God penetrates through our ideologies and aspirations to bring redemption and reformation. Integrating the whole gospel with every area of society rules out any naive notions that the gospel can be shouted from a distance; communication of the gospel must be personal, truthful, and relevant. John R. W. Stott has written,

Now it is comparatively easy to be faithful if we do not care about being contemporary, and easy also to be contemporary if we do not bother to be faithful. It is the search for a combination of truth and relevance which is exacting. Yet nothing else can save us from an insensitive loyalty to formulae and shibboleths on the one hand, and from a treasonable disloyalty to the revelation of God on the other. "Truth and timeliness" (to quote Bishop Phillips Brooks) make for communication, and without communication there is not evangelism, no actual sharing of the good news.[3]

There is no perfect time for integrating the way of Christ in the worldly arena. By the grace of God we must endure the resulting "cultural surgery" and ensuing tension with the world. But the "pain" is not to be compared to the benefits we have and will have in Christ. The Apostle's words ought to be our words.

. . . I count all things to be loss in view of the surpassing value of knowing Christ Jesus my Lord, for whom I have suffered the loss of all things, and count them but rubbish in order that I may gain Christ [Philippians 3:8, NASB].

For I consider that the sufferings of this present time are not worthy to be compared with the glory that is to be revealed to us [Romans 8:18, NASB].

When the auto mechanic wants to overhaul an engine, he has the advantage of shutting off the motor; but it is a different story for the surgeon. The body's life support systems must continue to function. If the heart can no longer pump blood through the circulation system, a machine must be employed to do the job. If the lungs can no longer supply oxygen to the body, a respirator must be used. Culture is more like a living organism than a motor. The "adaptive system" never ceases. If we are waiting for an ideal time to put Christ first in our lives, we can be assured that it will never come. The only perfect time we will ever have to secure the family, establish our priorities, show compassion to our neighbor, and obey Christ's call to global responsibility is *today*. If the "sons of this age" can be shrewd in their manipulation of culture then the "sons of light" ought to be wise in their penetration of culture (Luke 16:8). Jesus laid it out for us.

Behold, I send you out as sheep in the midst of wolves; therefore be shrewd as serpents, and innocent as doves [Matthew 10:16, NASB].

Guided by the Word and Spirit of God, the new reformation for which we seek is the reality needed most in our modern culture. Who will confront needy men and women with the truth and love of Christ? Who will have the courage and the compassion to be God's called out community in a fallen world? Will it be the church of culture with its christ of appeal and christ of conformity or the true Christ, Lord of all, Savior and the coming King; the Christ of the earthly cross and the heavenly throne?

Christ in you, the hope of glory [Colossians 1:27, NASB].

NOTES

CHAPTER 1, *The New Mentality*
1. Elton Trueblood, *Company of the Committed* (New York: Harper & Row, 1961), p. 90.

CHAPTER 2, *Who Is Christ? What Is Culture?*
1. H. Richard Niebuhr, *Christ and Culture* (New York: Harper, 1956), p. 32.
2. *Ibid.*, p. 33.
3. *Ibid.*, p. 3.
4. Jacques Ellul, *False Presence of the Kingdom* (New York: Seabury, 1972), p. 113.
5. Niebuhr, *Christ and Culture*, p. 7, quoted from Gibbon, *The Decline and Fall of the Roman Empire* (New York: Modern Library, 1932), vol. 1, p. 446.
6. John R. Stott, *Christ the Controversialist* (Downers Grove, IL: Inter-Varsity, 1970), p. 17.

CHAPTER 3, *Jesus Christ and the Whole Man*
1. C. S. Lewis, *Mere Christianity* (Glasgow: Collins, 1978), p. 180.
2. Alvin Toffler, *Future Shock* (New York: Bantam Books, 1970), p. 97.
3. Truman Douglass, *The New World of Urban Man* (Philadelphia: United Church Press, 1965), p. 51.

CHAPTER 4, *The Roman Milieu: Then As Now*
1. M. Rostovtzeff, *The Social and Economic History of the Roman Empire*, 2nd ed. (New York: Oxford University Press, 1951), p. 69.
2. Jules Toutain, *The Economic Life of the Ancient World* (New York: A. A. Knopf, 1930), p. 320.
3. Suetonius, *The Twelve Caesars*, trans. Robert Groves (Boston: Penguin Books, 1957), p. 178.
4. Tacitus, *The Annals*, trans. A. J. Church and W. J. Brodribb (Saaler and Brown Ltd.), bk. 14, sect. 44, pp. 257, 258.

5. Paul Maier, "The Infant Massacre: History or Myth?" *Christianity Today,* 19 December 1975.
6. C. K. Barrett, *The New Testament Background* (New York: Harper and Row, 1956), p. 91.
7. Cyril E. Robinson, *A History of Rome* (New York: Thomas Crowell, 1935), p. 301.
8. F. F. Bruce, *New Testament History* (New York: Doubleday, 1972), pp. 281, 282.
9. Harold Mattingly, *Christianity in the Roman Empire* (New York: Norton and Co., 1967), p. 12.
10. F. R. Cowell, *Everyday Life in Ancient Rome* (London: Batsford Ltd., 1961), pp. 19, 32.
11. M. F. Unger, *Archeology and the New Testament* (Grand Rapids: Zondervan, 1962), pp. 319, 320.
12. Seneca, *Moral Essays,* trans. John Basore (New York: Putnam's Sons, Loeb Library), vol. 1, p. 375.
13. M. F. Unger, *Archeology,* p. 200.
14. F. F. Bruce, *New Testament History,* p. 263.
15. Charles F. Pfeiffer, ed., *The Biblical World* (Grand Rapids: Baker, 1966), p. 44.
16. M. F. Unger, *Archeology,* p. 243.
17. M. C. Tenney, *New Testament Times* (Grand Rapids: Eerdmans, 1965), p. 272.

CHAPTER 5, *The Technological Tower of Babel*
1. Daniel J. Boorstin, "Tomorrow: The Republic of Technology," *Time,* 17 January 1977, p. 38.
2. Will Herberg (quoted by Gary Hardway, *Christianity Today,* 27 February 1976, p. 13).
3. Boorstin, "Tomorrow," p. 38.
4. *Ibid.*, p. 38.
5. Jacques Ellul, *The Meaning of the City* (Grand Rapids: Eerdmans, 1970), p. 16.
6. Toffler, *Future Shock,* p. 204.
7. Boorstin, "Tomorrow," p. 38.
8. Walter R. Hearn, "Whole People and Half Truths," *The Scientist and Ethical Decision,* ed. Charles Hatfield (Downers Grove, IL: Inter-Varsity, 1973), pp. 94, 95.
9. Toffler, *Future Shock*, p. 217.
10. Thomas Leale, *A Homiletic Commentary: Genesis* (New York: Funk and Wagnalls, 1893), p. 205.
11. August J. Kling, "Men of Science/Men of Faith," *His,* May 1976, pp. 26-31.
12. cf. Henry Stob, "Christian Ethics and Scientific Control," *The Scientist and Ethical Decision,* ed. Charles Hatfield (Downers Grove, IL: Inter-Varsity, 1973), p. 5.
13. Mark Hatfield, *Between a Rock and a Hard Place* (New York: Pocket Books, 1977), p. 166.

CHAPTER 6, *The Media*
1. George Gerbner and Larry Gross, "The Scary World of T.V.'s Heavy Viewer," *Psychology Today,* April 1976, p. 42.
2. Neil Harris, "How We Keep in Touch," *Time,* 16 February, 1976, p. 70.

3. Robert Hargreaves, *Superpower: A Portrait of America in the 70's* (New York: St. Martin's Press, Inc., 1973), p. 449.
4. Toffler, *Future Shock*, p. 167.
5. Edwin Kiesler, Jr., "T.V. Violence: What Can Parents Do?" *Better Homes and Gardens*, September 1975, p. 4.
6. Gerbner and Gross, "The Scary World of T.V.'s Heavy Viewer," p. 89.
7. Max Gunther, "All That T.V. Violence: Why Do We Love/Hate It?" *TV Guide*, 6 November 1976.
8. Toffler, *Future Shock*, p. 154.
9. Harris, "How We Keep in Touch," p. 70.
10. *Ibid.*, p. 70.
11. Unwin, quoted by Donald Drew, *Images of Man* (Downers Grove, IL: Inter-Varsity, 1974), p. 23.
12. Hargreaves, *Superpower*, p. 431.
13. Quoted by Hargreaves, *Superpower*, p. 431.
14. Kenneth Curtis, "How the Television Culture Has Become Our Real Religion," *Eternity*, November 1976, pp. 14, 15.
15. *Ibid.*, p. 60.
16. Joe Bayly, *The Gospel Blimp* (Grand Rapids: Zondervan, 1960).
17. Hargreaves, *Superpower*, p. 430.
18. Ellul, *False Presence*, pp. 65-68.

CHAPTER 7, *Materialism: The Endless Crave*
1. Alex Inkeles and David H. Smith, *Becoming Modern* (Cambridge, MA: Harvard University Press, 1974), p. 12.
2. *Ibid.*, p. 11.
3. Josif Ton, "The Socialist Quest of the New Man," *Christianity Today*, 26 March 1976.
4. W. Herbert Scott, "The Christian's Position: Above or Beside the Needy?" *World Vision*, July/August 1975, p. 16.
5. Dietrich Bonhoeffer, *The Cost of Discipleship* (New York: Macmillan, 1963), p. 195.
6. *Ibid.*, p. 195.

CHAPTER 8, *The Answers We Don't Give*
1. Walter Rauschenbusch, *Christianity and the Social Crisis* (New York: Harper and Row, 1964), p. 162.
2. "Jesus the Liberator," *Time*, 1 September 1975, p. 58.
3. Kenneth L. Woodward, "The Battle of the Bible," *Newsweek* 8 November 1976, p. 110.
4. Hargreaves, *Superpower*, p. 496.
5. Mark Hatfield, "Celebrating the Year of Liberation," *Christianity Today*, 26 March 1976, p. 13.
6. Robert H. Schuller, *Your Church Has Possibilities* (Glendale, CA: Regal Books, 1974), p. 117.
7. Ronald J. Sider, *Rich Christians in an Age of Hunger* (Downers Grove, IL: Inter-Varsity, 1977), pp. 105, 106.
8. Gary Lautens, "It's Our Duty to Live Beyond Our Means," *Toronto Star*, 30 March 1977.

CHAPTER 9, *Will the Family Survive?*
1. Philippe Ariès (interviewed by Jacques Mousseau), "The Family Prison of Love," *Psychology Today*, August 1975, p. 58.

2. *Ibid.,* p. 58.
3. William Willimon, "Marriage As a Subversive Activity," *Christianity Today,* 18 February 1977, p. 16.
4. Ariès, "Family Prison of Love," p. 58.
5. J. R. Stott, *Divorce* (Downers Grove, IL: Inter-Varsity, 1973), p. 14.
6. Willimon, "Marriage," p. 16.
7. Toffler, *Future Shock,* pp. 251, 252.
8. John M. Batteau, "Sexual Differences: A Cultural Convention?" *Christianity Today,* 8 July 1977, p. 10.
9. Quoted by Dr. Everett Koop, *The Right to Live; The Right to Die* (Wheaton, IL: Tyndale House, 1976), p. 36.
10. George W. Knight III, "Male and Female Related He Them," *Christianity Today,* 9 April 1976, p. 15.
11. Elisabeth Elliot Leitch, "A Christian View of Women's Liberation" (address delivered at Wheaton College Honors Convocation, 2 May 1975).
12. Ariès, "Family Prison of Love," p. 56.
13. Urie Bronfenbrenner (interviewed by Susan Byrne), "Nobody Home: The Erosion of the American Family," *Psychology Today,* May 1977, p. 45
14. *Ibid.,* p. 46.
15. Robert Coles, "Growing Up in America—Then and Now," *Time,* 29 December 1975, p. 29.
16. "Family: New Breed Vs. the Old," *Time,* 2 May 1977, p. 76.
17. Coles, "Growing Up in America," p. 29.
18. Edith Schaeffer, *What Is A Family?* (Old Tappan, NJ: Revell, 1975), p. 74.
19. *Ibid.,* p. 83.
20. *Ibid.,* p. 43.

CHAPTER 10, *Missions: A Way of Life*
1. John R. Stott, *The Christian Mission in the Modern World* (Downers Grove, IL: Inter-Varsity, 1975), p. 21.
2. Bonhoeffer, *The Cost of Discipleship,* p. 21.
3. Louis Luzbetak, *The Church and Cultures* (Techny, IL: Divine Word Publishers, 1963), p. 306.
4. Paul Rees, *World Vision,* October 1973, p. 23.
5. Luzbetak, *The Church and Cultures,* p. 97.
6. *Ibid.,* p. 99.
7. *Ibid.,* p. 158.
8. Don Richardson, *Peace Child* (Glendale, CA: Regal, 1974), p. 8.
9. *Ibid.,* p. 10.
10. Eugene A. Nida, *Customs and Cultures* (New York: Harper).
11. Luzbetak, *The Church and Cultures,* pp. 190, 248.
12. Stephen Neill, "The Best Investment," *Decision,* October 1976, p. 4.
13. *Ibid.,* p. 4.
14. Rachel Saint, "We Are Giving Them Back Their Culture," *Christianity Today,* 2 January 1976, p. 15.

CHAPTER 11, *The New Reformation*
1. Ellul, *The False Presence*, p. 25.
2. Visser't Hooft, "Evangelism in the Neo-Pagan Situation," *International Review of Mission*, vol. LXIII, no. 249, January 1974, p. 84.
3. Stott, *The Christian Mission in the Modern World*, p. 43.